The

SECRET
SECOND
COMING

What If the Church Got It Wrong

PATRICIA DOYLE

Cover Design by 100Covers.com
Interior Design by FormattedBooks.com

For permission contact Patricia Doyle:
secondnewtestament@gmail.com

Names:	Doyle, Patricia (Patricia E.), author.
Title:	The secret second coming : what if the church got it wrong / Patricia Doyle.
Description:	[Tacoma, Washington]: [Hummingbird House Publishing], [2020] | Includes bibliographical references.
Identifiers:	ISBN: 978-1-7344657-1-6 (paperback) | 978-1-7344657-0-9 (eBook) | 978-1-7344657-2-3 (audiobook)
Subjects:	LCSH: Second Advent. | Jesus Christ (Spirit) | Holy Spirit. | God–Love. | Padgett, James E. (James Edward), 1852-1923. | Spirit writings. | Future life. | Bible and spiritualism. | Bible. New Testament–Criticism, interpretation, etc. | Channeling (Spiritualism) | Mediums–Religious aspects. | Bible. Revelation–Criticism, interpretation, etc. | Religion and science. | Prophecy–Christianity. | Near-death experience–Religious aspects. | Mysticism–Christianity.
Classification:	LCC: BF1311.J5 D69 2020 | DDC: 133.9/3--dc23

Dedicated to Jason and J.D.

My second coming will be as the still small voice that speaks to every man and tells him that love is the only thing that is necessary for him to have, and when he gets that in his soul, all the sins and hatred and desires for evil will pass away.

—Jesus

CONTENTS

Introduction IX

Chapter 1: Proof of Afterlife 1
Chapter 2: The Second Coming: Has It Already Happened? 13
Chapter 3: The Momentous Padgett Messages 25
Chapter 4: Revelation: Prophecy, Spiritualism, and Old
            Testament Influences 39
Chapter 5: New Testament Authority 57
Chapter 6: NDEs and OBEs 81
Chapter 7: Confirmations & Channeling 99
Chapter 8: A Spiritual Crucible 115
Chapter 9: What Would Jesus Say? 133
Chapter 10: The Divine Dare From Jesus 143

Conclusion 149
Bibliography 155
Appendix 163
About The Author 199
Invitation to Participate 201

INTRODUCTION

"All great truths begin as blasphemies."

—George Bernard Shaw, playwright and
Nobel laureate, b. 1856

"Extraordinary claims require extraordinary evidence."

—Carl Sagan, physicist and author, b. 1934

A TRANSFORMATION OF humanity is occurring from an event that happened one hundred years ago. Yet few people know about it. It is the world's most profound secret, hiding in plain sight, behind an invisible veil of disbelief. But that veil is about to disappear because the afterlife and communication with the dead are now established facts. Proven by scientists. Proven by attorneys.

It's not speculation. It is reality. It's only a matter of time for the knowledge to become known. The veils are being lifted at an accelerating pace. The rapidity of mass communication through the internet enables us to discover and absorb information at a faster rate than ever in the recorded history of humanity.

Over a thousand books are available about near-death experiences, written by people who have had NDEs, and by scientists and researchers studying them. These reports are only one source of evidence of the spirit world, the afterlife, and communication with the deceased. If you look at the evidence, the extensive and irrefutable proof is there. A skeptic is only someone who has not yet examined the proof.

A journey to discover secret documents with the power to spiritually awaken all of humanity was the central theme of the popular novel *Celestine Prophecy* by James Redfield. What if there *were* *real* documents as profound as the ancient documents in *Celestine Prophecy*, with the same transforming power?

Such documents *do* exist and many people alive today are living testimony to their miraculous existence. I am one and I will lead you to their discovery.

I have had out-of-body experiences, a near-death experience, and several meetings with the living spirit of Jesus. These occurred before and after learning about these documents, and they correlate with and corroborate them. In my first encounter with Jesus, he informed me that my destiny, if I chose to fulfill it, was to play a key role in the revealing of his second coming. Errors in the Bible needed correcting and humanity needed to understand the importance of obtaining God's Love. We, too, like Jesus, could accomplish a total transformation of our souls, even while still in mortal form.

———— ❧❧ ————

I was fortunate to grow up in a family that was open-minded about religion and accepted the existence of the spirit world. I was allowed, even encouraged, to attend any church I wanted, and to think for myself. As a young child, I was impressed by Jesus and how important he was to the world. He seemed to change everything, even the way we define our place in time.

I wanted to know all I could about this incredible person and his teachings. But the information in the Bible and what was being taught in the churches left me unsatisfied. This early desire and love for Jesus stayed with me, and led me to understand him as a dear brother and best friend. He guides us with his great love, as the greatest teacher of the highest truth available—the secret knowledge of connecting directly with God.

Have you ever wanted to know more about Jesus? Craved more? Have you ever wondered what Jesus was like as a child? Was he like other children? When did he first know what his calling was and how did he know? How does God answer prayer? The answer, revealed in this book, might surprise you.

We now have the answers to these questions, and more, straight from Jesus, through *psicografica* (spirit-to-mortal written communications), received in the early twentieth century. The medium was James Padgett, a Washington D.C. attorney and Methodist Sunday school teacher. He developed his mediumship and his soul to receive messages from the spirit of Jesus of Nazareth, but never received any money or fame for it.

Within these messages, Jesus reveals spiritual and Celestial secrets like the creation of the first parents and the progress of humanity; the nature of God, His qualities and attributes; Jesus' life and ministry; the distinction between the natural love and the Divine Love; the incarnation of the human soul; and the nature of the spirit world, spiritual progression, and communication. This material is easy to read and understand. And it transcends any particular religion or church because it ministers to the unchangeable laws of God.

The most authoritative information about Jesus and his mission would come from Jesus himself, right? So, wouldn't it be amazing and wonderful to have writings from Jesus? That is the promise of the exceptional Padgett messages—the most inspiring message ever offered to humanity, and yet the most secret!

I can hear you asking, *Why haven't we heard about this before? Why is it taking so long for this to become known?* I discuss several reasons throughout this book, but the biggest reason is because we were not ready. Human beings are resistant to change. It takes a long time for knowledge and discoveries to get passed down into the general population. It has to be gradual, one person at a time, until enough people have integrated the knowledge for a critical shift to occur. At that point the rate of acceptance becomes self-sustaining and accelerated. But some people will always resist, no matter what the truth is, no matter how much better it makes their lives.

We also have resistance to this material by established religion and science. Scientists with a materialistic worldview consider it to be impossible, but the unexpected existence of dark matter and the strange findings of quantum mechanics are enlightening these views.

Jesus' teachings rattled the religious and political powers of his time with a message so radical that he was murdered. His teachings were then diluted, distorted, and fabricated.

Jesus' contemporary teachings through James Padgett are still alien and threatening to many Christian religious orders. Their doctrine views the messages as heretical because of the connection with spiritualism, and they cite passages from the Old Testament that advise resistance to spiritualism. But Jesus himself was a spiritualist.

———— ⋙✻⋘ ————

The Lincoln Séance: Proof of Lincoln

My education in afterlife studies began in my early teens when I was first able to sense what felt like spirits in my bedroom at night. Not scary ghosts, but the presence of benevolent and comforting energies separate from myself. I wondered if I could somehow communicate with them. I tried to think of a method for doing this and came up with the idea of using a candle. Because of the etheric nature of the flame, I thought it could possibly be swayed by the spirits.

I sat alone on the floor with a lit candle in front of me, and thought of 'yes' and 'no' questions. I asked the spirits who were present to answer by manipulating the flame. If the answer was 'yes' they were to make the flame rise high. If the answer was 'no' they were to make the flame go low and almost flicker out. I started asking questions—and got results! But that was alone. Well, not really alone. *Was my mind playing tricks on me? Could I get it to happen with witnesses? Maybe some of my friends would be interested.*

My friends and I would often explore psychic and spiritual subjects. One activity we experimented with was levitation. It took six people: five levitators and one lucky levitatee, who would lie on the ground and rise to over the heads of the levitators, feeling light as a feather. We used only our forefingers, placed in strategic areas, with two people on each side, and one at the head. The person at the head prepared the levitatee by stroking her face with a circular feather touch, while cooing "light as a feather" and counting down from ten.

Then, on cue with the number one, the five levitators would synchronously lift their forefingers, with ease, while our friend floated to over six feet from the ground. Just ten fingers. To our amazement, it always worked. I experienced it many times from every position. We had no idea how it worked, only that it did. I still don't know, but I suspect there are links to hypnotism, precise timing, and the incredible strength of just a single finger. (Warren Travis, an early twentieth century strongman, lifted 560 pounds with one finger, on his 50th birthday.) It was exceptional fun. Especially for a teen who could not get enough when it came to topics related to the mysterious and unknown.

One night at a slumber party, I asked a small group of friends if they wanted to try communicating with spirits, like I had been doing alone. We went into a travel trailer and sat in a circle at the small table, holding hands, with a candle in the middle of the table. I did the same thing I had been doing in my bedroom, but when I started to get results again, I became uncomfortable. I wanted to make sure we would communicate with a good spirit, and not a bad one.

So, I asked for the spirit of Abraham Lincoln to come. The flame lengthened. When I asked if Abraham Lincoln was there, the flame rose even higher—this time not ambiguous. But this was not enough for me. Like humans sometimes pretend to be who they are not, I felt that this could be possible with a spirit too. So, I began to struggle mentally, trying to come up with a way for the spirit to prove it actually was Abraham Lincoln.

I don't recall whether I voiced any of this struggle, but the flame shot higher as a cold chill whipped through us. Our hands broke apart, and the friends across from me shrieked, pointing to the wall behind me. The image of Abraham Lincoln appeared on the wall, they said! I did not see it. When I turned, it was gone. But I felt the power. The whole environment changed. A cool wind had rushed through the small, enclosed room, as if a window were open. I also believe it happened because of the sincerity of my friends. They were good friends, with good moral character. It was not a joke. No one was laughing.

This had a profound effect on me. I decided to quit with séances because there was a lot of power that I didn't know how to control.

I didn't know what I was doing. Above all, I wanted assurance of protection from lower, negative influences.

It is still amazing to me that Abraham Lincoln manifested like that. I am very grateful for the experience. One thing it taught me was that it is okay to ask for proof, especially when dealing with spirits. It is important and necessary. I approached the subject with caution from then on, but with openness, because I had experienced its reality.

Part of my crucible of discernment for accepting information from mediums as being what is claimed, is proof—*evidential* mediumship. Specific details. Personal information or intimate matters known only by relatives or colleagues still on earth. Manifestation of personal characteristics. Dates, names, and details of the spirit's experiences on earth that can be verified as coming from no other source.

I have been studying and researching the afterlife for more than fifty-five years. I have read hundreds of books on after-death communication, channeling, and mediumship; spiritism, spiritualism, and seances; spirituality, spiritual growth, and transformation; spirit attachments, possession, and exorcisms; mysticism, apparitions, and mystical visions; NDEs, OBEs, and STEs; meditation, prayer, and transcendental experiences; clairaudience, clairsentience, and clairvoyance; God, Jesus, and angels; healers, healing research, and spiritual healing; and the scientific exploration of spirituality and consciousness research.

I have attended many conferences, experiential workshops, and retreats and have hosted spiritual retreats. While majoring in religion for three years at the University of Puget Sound in the early 1990s, I put the Padgett messages through strict academic challenges, which you will see in this book.

Volunteer work for transformational organizations has been a vital part of my life. As a youth, I was active in the Masonic-affiliated International Order of Rainbow for Girls, a charity-oriented organization that develops leadership through community service. I was eighteen when I rose to the office of Worthy Advisor, the highest office possible in a local chapter, a process that takes two and a half years.

In the early 1980s, I was active in Paramahansa Yogananda's Self-Realization Fellowship in Encinitas, California. At that time, I also engaged with the Erhard Seminar Training, through several of their leadership training programs. I was a top-performing logistics supervisor for dozens of EST symposiums.

Transcendental Meditation is a practice I began in 1968 during my first year of college at Washington State University. Quieting the mind, placing the conscious mind off to the side, has been an important practice. This useful exercise has served me well and taken on many variations, including visualization and meditation-in-action.

During my early twenties, I challenged God to prove to me that He existed. For years I received no answer to satisfy me. I drifted into becoming an agnostic, until October 1974, when God saved my life by intervening during an imminent stabbing. In a powerful and unmistakable way, He infused His Love into me and the entire environment, instantly reversing the threat. I immediately turned from an agnostic into someone blessed with unshakable faith in God. My challenge was finally answered with solid proof of the tangible existence of God and that God is Love. This propelled me into increasing periods of blissful at-one-ness with Him. And onto a path of service I could never have predicted. I gave my life completely to God on the day of my near-death experience, yearning to be always at-one with Him.

Two years after this faith-changing NDE, Jesus invited me to be part of the revealing of his second coming. Six years later, when introduced to the messages from Jesus through James Padgett that represent his second coming, Jesus called on me again (for the second time) to verify them. Two years later, I was appointed president of the Foundation dedicated to these important messages.

It is a great privilege to testify on the power of God and the spiritually transformative experiences that connect me to these documents and Jesus' second coming. My story is remarkable. Padgett's story is astounding. Jesus' story is revolutionary and phenomenal. And now has a powerful and Loving second chapter!

-------→≫≪←-------

The Longing for Truth

We all depend on truth, and without it, we suffer as individuals and as a society. Truth is important in all relationships, as there can be no trust without it. Many of us engage in a long and perilous quest for spiritual truth. It is a huge act of faith that Absolute Truth exists and that we can find it.

Before going any further, I want to acknowledge that the Bible does contain many truths, and enough to enable us to reach divinity through God's Love if understood and applied. Luke, of the New Testament, makes this vital point in a message delivered through Padgett. But, he also points out: "There are so many things taught therein as truths, which are just the opposite of truth, that they make it difficult for men to discern and apply the truth, and comprehend the will of God with respect to men, and the destinies that must be theirs according as they follow and obey that will or do not do so." (Padgett, 1958: I:154)

One such untruth is the vicarious atonement. Jesus emphasizes and writes *repeatedly* that his death on the cross *did not* and *has not ever* forgiven anyone. The atonement is false and is a harmful belief. It's more difficult to say no to abuse when influenced by a teaching that demonstrates that suffering at the hands of others is the highest form of love. The way traditional Christianity has interpreted the suffering of Jesus has made it difficult for abuse victims to find healing. Instead, abuse becomes tolerated and perpetuated with a twisted religious belief that teaches that suffering is love. *"For God so loved the world, that he gave his only begotten son... "* The only way to true salvation is through God's love, and there is no suffering involved in that experience at all.

We need redemption from false beliefs and erroneous doctrines and dogmas. We all long for truth—the kind of truth that removes superstition and errors from spiritual teachings. Truth that will accord with reason. Faith and reason should co-exist. Jesus writes:

> Humanity is now longing for the truth of the Father, and their longings must be satisfied. No longer will form and ceremony and the mere declarations of the churches as to what God has provided for his children and what the churches have provided be sufficient to satisfy. The mind as well as the credulity of men must be considered, and when the teachings of the churches are against reason and the knowledge of spiritual laws which men may learn, these souls which hunger and thirst for God's love and the way to obtain it must be satisfied. (Padgett, 1958: II:93)

False beliefs and teachings bring consequences, whether we are aware of them or not. Jesus writes about the beliefs of a mission preacher who taught that only the converted were sons of God. Jesus calls this a "damnable and harmful" doctrine, because it causes many souls to give up hope of becoming better. The preacher had Divine Love in his soul, and was sincere in his seeking, but his beliefs and teachings were wrong. This retarded not only the development of his own soul and advancement toward the Celestial Kingdom, but the progress of his entire congregation.

His mental beliefs, coming from the Bible and Christian theology teachers, were firmly rooted and sincere, but still false. He suffered immensely. "Ignorance," writes Jesus, "while it will not relieve him from its consequences, and neither will it invoke the penalties of the law that apply to the willful deceiver or teacher of false doctrines, yet neither will it excuse him or relieve him from the penalties of that law which demands the truth, and only the truth to be believed and taught." Jesus continues: "He will have to get rid of these false beliefs, even though he may have some of the divine in his soul; for whenever there exists untruth in belief in the heart and soul of man, to that extent it interferes with the inflowing of the Love into and the progression of that soul towards perfect unity with the Father." (Padgett, 1958: I:30-31)

"Truth is of itself a fact," states Jesus. "It can have no affiliation with untruth, no matter that untruth is the result of ignorance, for all untruth is the result of ignorance, and must be eradicated from the hearts of men before there can be that harmony between God and man which the very nature of truth itself requires." (Padgett, 1958: I:30-31)

An Orthodox minister wrote through Padgett about passing over with his orthodox beliefs. He was disappointed that Jesus did not greet him and bring him into the presence of God to receive approval as a faithful and obedient child. When instructed that his beliefs were wrong, he was shocked. He became doubtful of everything as he thought about the long life he had given to the cultivation and establishment of these beliefs. He became resentful and hardened. He refused to believe in anything, and the realization of his deception made him rebellious. He almost hated spirits and God.

After a while, his spirit friends told him that indulging in these thoughts was harmful. It would prevent him from learning the real way to happiness and salvation. The longer he indulged in these feelings of resentment about deception, the greater would be his stagnation and the darker his surroundings would become.

He had to learn that all things obeyed the unchangeable laws of God. Beliefs do not matter, unless those beliefs are true. He remained in darkness for some time, refusing to believe what he heard. It is not easy to get rid of the beliefs of a lifetime on earth, even though the surroundings of the spirit world show that these beliefs are false. Belief is a very important factor in determining the destiny of the soul. Many come to the spirit world with the wrong belief in Jesus' vicarious atonement, and it is a stumbling block to their progress.

John, the disciple of Jesus, writes, "the pity of it all is that mortals for all these long years have believed that they were saved by his sacrifice and blood, and by such belief have never come any nearer to the Master or in at-onement with the Father." (Padgett, 1958: I:224)

How is it fair that our salvation depends on the belief that Jesus died on the cross for our sins? It does not make sense. It isn't fair and it isn't right. A just and loving God would not have a prerequisite like that. What if you live as a Pygmy in the remote Congo jungle? The Pygmies have never heard of Jesus, yet they seem to have a very close relationship with God.

If it were true that Jesus had to die on the cross for our sins to be forgiven, then how did the woman who anointed Jesus' feet with her tears and dried them with her hair receive her forgiveness? Jesus was still alive when he pronounced, *"Your faith has saved you; go in peace." (Luke 7:48-50)*

In the messages through Padgett, we learn that this whole idea of Jesus dying on the cross for our sins is untrue. And that God's truths all make sense. There is no secret or mystery that we are not supposed to understand. Even the "mystery" of the Christian Trilogy (three gods in one: Father, Son, and Holy Ghost) is revealed. It's no mystery at all, but a lack of understanding.

"The great gift of God to man was not Jesus, but the potentiality of obtaining the Divine Love of the Father and thus becoming divine and fitted to reside in the mansions of the Kingdom of Heaven," writes John, Jesus' beloved disciple. "And thus Jesus became the resurrection and the life and brought immortality to light. He is the savior of man by his living and his teachings, for he was the first to receive this Divine Love and to become divine himself." (Padgett, 1958: I:224-225)

The Second Death

Now is the time to learn about and absorb Jesus' teachings because the day will come when the Celestial Heavens will close. This is known as the second death, and no one knows when this will happen, not even Jesus:

> Until the time comes when the Father shall withdraw from man and spirit the privilege of obtaining this Divine Love and essence, which time will bring the second death, these spirits and all spirits and mortals will have the opportunity of seeking for and finding the way to the Celestial spheres and immortality. But after that time this privilege will no longer exist, and then those spirits and mortals who have not found and followed the way of that privilege… will have no assurance of immortality, or even continuous life, and that dissatisfaction and longing for something unknown, will be theirs. (Padgett, 1958: I:89)

Jesus' disciple John also writes about the second death:

... so long as the Father requires his great truths to be taught and men's souls saved from the effect of the great fall... our work will continue. But sometime our work on earth, as well as in the spirit spheres, will cease, and then our homes in the Celestial spheres will be our only places of labor and love. The Kingdom will be completed—the door of the Heavenly Kingdom closed, and the angelic laborers become separated from the spiritual or perfect man. Such is the decree. And as the Father desires all men to become at-one with Him in His divinity of Love, we must work until the great day of the consummation of the Kingdom arrives... (Padgett, 1958: I:154-155)

Why not choose the path that leads to divinity and union with God? A path that makes immortality a certainty, instead of one that leads to limitation of progress and happiness? No other path will bring our soul into union with God, and make our nature divine. No sacraments of baptism and no ceremonies of the church will accomplish it, but may actually hinder the soul from developing in God's Love. This Love is waiting for all humanity, no matter where they live, and they can receive God's Love even though they have never heard of Jesus.

All men and spirits will have the opportunity to accept God's greatest gift of Divine Love before the closing of the Celestial Kingdom, but many will not accept it. We must exercise our free will, as God never forces anything on us. The variety of beliefs and teachings on Earth about the meaning of the second death will cause many to neglect to exercise this privilege. When the Kingdom closes, the gift will be withdrawn again, as it was for the first parents when they rejected the privilege, and those who have not chosen God's Love will experience the second death. Not death in the sense of annihilation or condemnation to eternal punishment, but the withdrawing of the presence of God in the soul. (Padgett, 1958: II:275) (To read the full message from Jesus, see the Appendix, *Destiny of Man Without Divine Love Who Dies Only with Natural Love and Belief in the Creeds and Dogmas of the Churches.*)

————※————

What do you want this world to be like for your children and grand-children? More peaceful, loving, and harmonious? Want to be part of the new reformation in Christian thinking? Or at least know about it? Ready to grasp the truth about spiritual things? Aspire for and obtain a higher course of living? We have the power to decrease suffering and create a more enlightened world for ourselves and future gen-erations. We now have new knowledge about the second coming of Jesus—directly from Jesus, clearing the confusion of religious falsity and replacing it with the freedom of truth and Love.

There is no reason to be in the dark anymore, and every reason to walk in the light of a world ruled by truth and Love. Not by lies and fear. This is not only possible, but inevitable, once we accept the spirit world and integrate these contemporary teachings from Jesus and his Celestial colleagues. The promise is nothing less than Heaven on Earth—a new alliance of humanity—attainable because we can be connected to God, like Jesus, through Love.

————※————

"The world is full of magical things patiently waiting for our wits to grow sharper."

—Bertrand Russell, Nobel laureate philosopher
and author, b. 1872

CHAPTER 1

PROOF OF AFTERLIFE

"The day science begins to study non-physical phenomena, it will make more progress in one decade than in all the previous centuries of its existence."

—Nikola Tesla, inventor and engineer, b. 1856

WE ARE IN the midst of a great revolution in our understanding of ourselves as spiritual beings having a spiritual experience in the physical plane. We are awakening to the invisible world that's all around us, the world that makes up most of reality. Today there is no longer any argument that many things exist even though we can't see them with our physical eyes. X-rays. Gamma rays. Ultraviolet light. Infrared light. Wind. Microwaves. Radio waves. Television waves....

Pioneers of radio and television, Guglielmo Marconi, Thomas Edison, John Logie Baird, Sir William Crookes, and Sir Oliver Lodge, were so certain of the reality of spirit correspondence that they were using their expert skills to establish it. (Zammit, 2013: 157) At the time of his death, Marconi was reportedly developing an electronic system to communicate with the deceased. (Zammit, 2013: 157)

A long list of hundreds of eminent scientists, professors, scholars, and doctors have studied the afterlife. They were skeptical at first, but after thorough investigation, became convinced. Among the scientists interested in paranormal studies are chemist and physicist William Crookes; evolutionary biologist Alfred Russel Wallace; physicist Sir Oliver Lodge; physician and author Arthur Conan Doyle; and Nobel Prize winners in physics, Marie and Pierre Curie. The Curies were fascinated with mediumistic séances, taking part in forty-three scientific experiments at the Institut Général Psychologique of Paris, from 1905 to 1907. They were looking for the source of the secret energy behind radioactivity through Spiritualism. (Champlain, 2013: 69)

Many modern physicists are not satisfied with materialist science because it can't account for the evidence coming from paranormal phenomena. Dozens of physicists have written books urging acceptance of a new worldview, which includes psychic phenomena and the existence of the afterlife.

Two of the hottest topics in physics today, entanglement and nonlocality, contradict assumptions of classical physics. Classical physics is concerned with the normal scale of observation. Entanglement, at the microscopic level of quantum physics, is a phenomenon so strange that physicist Albert Einstein described it as "spooky action at a distance." Entangled particles remain connected so that actions performed on one affect the other. And they 'know' about each other's state immediately, even when separated by great distances (potentially even billions of light years).

This is where nonlocality comes in. It does not matter where the particles are located. They still know what is going on with each other. Nonlocality is a quality of entanglement, making them, well, entangled. They are facts of quantum systems which have been repeatedly demonstrated in scientific experiments. These facts contradict the Principle of Locality (in classical physics) which states that distant objects can't have direct influence on one another—that an object is influenced directly only by its immediate surroundings.

Entanglement and nonlocality suggest that "separate" parts of the universe are actually connected in intimate and immediate ways.

The Victorious Zammits

Victor Zammit, a retired lawyer, and his wife, Wendy Zammit, a professional psychologist, have compiled three decades of research on the afterlife into a brilliant book, *A Lawyer Presents the Evidence for the Afterlife*. This bestseller presents evidence that Victor Zammit calls "credible, repeatable and admissible in a court of law." (Zammit, 2013: Introduction) The bibliography has 389 books cited.

With his background as an attorney and his university training in the scientific method, psychology, and history, Victor makes the following bold statement: "I have come to the irreversible conclusion that there is a great body of evidence which absolutely proves the case for the afterlife. In fact I am stating that the evidence taken as a whole constitutes overwhelming and irrefutable proof for the existence of the afterlife." (Zammit, 2013: 1)

No one has been able to disprove the extensive verification presented by the Zammits. They issued a standing challenge for any materialist or skeptic to dispute the evidence which would be "technically admissible in the Supreme Court of the United States, the House of Lords in England, the High Court of Australia and in every civilized legal jurisdiction around the world." (Zammit, 2013: 1-2) As of 2018, the last time I heard them speak on the subject, no one has taken them up on the dare.

We have found that the materialist closed-minded skeptics who oppose the existence of psychic phenomena and the afterlife have not done their homework. They simply have not read, as we have, volume after volume of first-hand accounts by the greatest minds of science who were all initially highly skeptical before they started their own personal investigations. (Zammit, 2013: 14)

"For the purpose of the record," write the Zammits, "no genius materialist, no skeptic, no disbeliever, no scoffer scientist has ever written a book explaining why there is not and cannot be an afterlife. No closed-minded skeptic has ever rebutted the afterlife evidence showing where, when, how and why the afterlife evidence cannot be valid." But the opposite is true—hundreds of eminent scientists have accepted the afterlife after investigating it seriously, and many of them have written books.

Debunkers have opposed every discovery and invention throughout history. One example given by the Zammits includes skeptics who stated it was "absolute rubbish that television waves could produce a picture." And Edison's recording was accused of being a fraud, a case of ventriloquism, by a fellow scientist from the French Academy of Sciences. (Zammit, 2013: 241)

Victor Zammit is qualified to examine the credibility of witnesses. As an attorney, it has been part of his profession to examine their reputations, character, stability, and motives. Wendy and Victor also spent more than fifteen months, on a weekly basis, investigating David Thompson. Thompson is a rare *physical* medium who produces Independent Voice, not coming from the mouth of the medium, but from a materialized spirit who becomes solid enough to walk around the room. The Zammits became part of David's Circle of the Silver Cord and continued to sit with him for another five years.

I observed David Thompson's mediumship at a symposium in 2017 in Scottsdale, Arizona. David, muffled with a gag, sits bound to a heavy wooden chair with his hands and feet secured by cable ties removable only by wire cutters. David, along with all the sitters, are thoroughly searched before the sitting. Everything in the room is thoroughly checked. Windows and doors sealed.

The results have been irrefutable. For more information about Thompson, you can go to the Circle of the Silver Cord website and see video testimonials. Thousands of people have attended his séances in the United States, England, Australia, Germany, Spain, and Switzerland over the past thirty years.

The Zammits' book is not religious. They clearly state: "The afterlife has nothing to do with religion or with beliefs or superstition. The afterlife is now scientifically established. Those who refuse to investigate or rebut the voluminous available evidence have no technical right or authority to deny its existence or to make any valid comments about it." (Zammit, 2013: 228) So it is up to each of us to either accept the evidence, or not. The astounding proof is there, and it is so important to our well-being as a society.

"There is so much evidence for the afterlife which is objective, stunning in its consistency, and which taken as a whole amounts to technical, irrefutable proof," write the Zammits. "Materialists, debunkers, and closed-minded skeptics have NOT given a credible alternative explanation for any of the above-demonstrated afterlife phenomena. In the absence of a credible alternative explanation, Society has no alternative but to accept that the afterlife exists and that we will all inevitably experience it." (Zammit, 2013: 230)

The Zammits offer several reasons why cynics and skeptics refuse to accept the evidence:

- **Cognitive dissonance**: When confronted with information that does not match a cherished belief, the cynic will try to reduce their discomfort by rationalizing firmly-held beliefs and by extreme denial.

- **Cathexis**: An extreme attachment, like superglue, to a belief. It is powerful and unconscious. Neither logic nor evidence can undo it.
- **Neurolinguistic programming**: Some people, when faced with information that is contradictory to their cherished beliefs, will delete that information from their consciousness. They go into complete denial.
- **Environmental programming and conditioning**: We are all shaped by our environments and the way we were raised. This affects our perception. We all have biases, whether we are aware of them or not.
- **Established neural pathways:** Can prevent new information from getting absorbed and decoded by the brain.

Some people are in denial because their status, power, and livelihood depend on their established beliefs. Other resistances to change come from cognitive biases inherent in our nature as humans:

- **Information bias**: We look for information to support our beliefs.
- **Confirmation bias**: We tend to only hear what confirms our beliefs.
- **Negativity bias**: We tend to place more weight on negative information and experiences instead of positive ones.
- **Anchoring bias**: We rely too heavily on one piece of information when deciding.
- **Band-Wagon Effect**: We tend to believe or do what others do. (Diamandis, 2012)

The Smile from Tesla

Instrumental Transcommunication (ITC) is an effective tool for communication with the deceased through electronic voice phenomena (EVP) and trans images. Sonia Rinaldi, a pioneering ITC researcher from Brazil, records voices of spirits speaking to their mortal loved ones. She has thousands of audio recordings of EVP, and video recordings with images appearing on the wall. She has reunited over 166 families with loved ones on the other side.

There is a concerted effort in the spirit world to bring this technology to us. Sonia's procedure is clearly defined. She has been working with a team of researchers, scientists, and engineers in the spirit realm, including Edison, Einstein, and Tesla. Edison, regarded as the first person to think of ITC, was not able to realize his vision while mortal.

At the 2018 Afterlife Research and Education Institute Symposium, Rinaldi reported that in the years 2016–18, a tremendous expansion occurred in the Interdimensional Net that makes ITC possible—Tesla joined the South Transmission Station in Brazil with the North Transmission Station in the U.S. Australia is also part of the expansion. The quality of images and recordings has taken a quantum leap. Rinaldi has received hundreds of remarkable trans images, including a smiling image of Tesla.

Katarina Mirkovic was the first parent to receive messages from her son through ITC with Sonia. An image appeared over her hair in one photo and another photo had a transfiguration on top of Katarina's face. Rev. Sheri Migdol received a very clear picture of her son. The first parents to talk to their deceased son through ITC also had an image produced on film. When the mom joyfully recognized the image, he moved his head! You can see some of this evidence at http://www.afterliferesearch.org/arei-initiatives-instrumental-transcommunication/, or look online for the Rinaldi Institute of Advanced Research in Instrumental Transcommunication.

The Catholic Church has even taken a favorable interest in EVP. The Zammits present four and a half pages of evidence in their book about the Church's encouragement of EVP investigation. Many Christians may find this surprising, but the Vatican has been positive and sympathetic, giving permission for its own priests to conduct research into the voices. (Zammit, 2013)

Afterlife Symposiums

The Afterlife Research and Education Institute (AREI) is a nonprofit service organization dedicated to helping afterlife researchers, educators, and practitioners advance their work. The Institute is endeavoring to make afterlife communication common. AREI holds that we are eternal beings, that death is a normal transition to the next stage of life, and that we are here to grow together in love.

I attended three annual symposiums sponsored by AREI in 2015–2018 in Scottsdale, Arizona. It is gratifying to see the growing interest in these symposiums. The first one I attended in 2015 had three hundred attendees; in 2017, there were 530 attendees; and in 2018, there were over eight hundred—more than doubling attendance in three years. This three-day event features inspiring and entertaining presentations by healing practitioners, hypnotherapists, authors, psychologists, NDE and OBE (out-of-body) experiencers, professors, ministers, metaphysical and spiritual explorers, and ... lawyers. Wendy and Victor Zammit are founding members of the board of directors.

Speaking of lawyers, again, the AREI symposiums have always included Mark Anthony as a keynote speaker. Mark Anthony, known as the Psychic Lawyer, is a famous evidential medium and author of the bestselling book *Evidence of Eternity: Communicating with Spirits for Proof of the Afterlife.* He gave an entertaining and engaging presentation on "Rulers Royals Spirits and Psychics" at the 2018 Symposium. A high point was his telling about an incident at the White House involving Winston Churchill, who was staying in the Lincoln bedroom during World War II. Churchill, naked after hopping out of a long bath, walked into the main bedroom where he saw Abraham Lincoln leaning on the fireplace. The two looked at each other, and Churchill supposedly said, "Good evening, Mr. President. You seem to have me at a disadvantage." Lincoln's ghost smiled a little and faded away. After that, Churchill refused to stay in the Lincoln bedroom.

Craig Hogan, president of the board of directors of AREI, gave the 2017 audience a sample of his Afterlife Connections procedure. This self-guided technique is available free at selfguided. spiritualunderstanding.org. It teaches people "how to guide themselves into a connection with loved ones on the next plane of life." His demonstration gave us a brief experience. Before his work for AREI, Craig was a professor of business communications at three universities; curriculum and training administrator at two universities and a medical school; and director of his own online business writing school.

I had the pleasure of meeting Sandra Champlain, the international best-selling author of *We Don't Die: A Skeptic's Discovery of Life After Death*, at the 2017 and 2018 symposiums. Her radio program, We Don't Die Radio, has over ten thousand daily listeners. I sat near her at one of the presentations at the 2017 symposium. Before the session started, she unconsciously channeled to me that my son's surgery would go well. I immediately knew this was a gift from God, as his well-being was very much on my soul. I needed the reassurance. His first surgery was difficult, and afterward, he suffered for many days, choking, barely able to breathe. I was coming home to his second surgery for the same issue. Now I could face it with the confidence that comes only from faith, and pass this faith on to my son. His surgery went well.

Gary E. Schwartz, professor of psychology, medicine, neurology, psychiatry, and surgery at the University of Arizona, presented scientific proof of mediumship at the 2017 symposium. He and his colleagues (on both sides of the veil) have been working diligently for years to bring a technology and a device they call the SoulPhone into creation. With this device, you would be able to "call" a loved one from the spirit world, like making a telephone call mortal to mortal.

Susanne Wilson, also on the AREI board, is a validated medium. She participated in controlled scientific research with Professor Gary Schwartz, as well as other scientists and researchers. Her book, *Soul Smart: What the Dead Teach Us About Spirit Communication,* teaches us how to communicate with our loved ones and guides on the other side.

Suzanne Wilson, Craig Hogan, and others, are teaching people how to be mediums by using out-of-body experiences and visualization meditation to meet loved ones at a predetermined time and location.

There are many different ways spirits can make their presence known to us through our five senses. Sometimes we can feel their touch, hear their voices, smell something related to them, or sense their presence. Sometimes we can actually see them, not with our inner vision only, but with our physical eyes. Sometimes we see a two-dimensional image, like a photo. We are particularly sensitive when in the hypnagogic or hypnopompic state, before going to sleep, or before waking. It is common to have a dream visit from a loved one. The spirits also use electrical devices such as televisions, radios, computers, clocks, lights going on and off, beeping noises from a stove, etc. to get our attention or deliver a message.

We receive messages and influences from the spirit world in nearly everything we do, whether conscious of it or not. It is important to become more aware of this and learn to be in communication with our loved ones on the other side, and, especially, the Celestials.

The Afterlife Investigations, a documentary film about the Scole Experimental Group, provides excellent proof of communication with the spirit world. Using a new and unique approach, renowned scientists participated in a serious study to produce a huge number and variety of tangible phenomena to make the scientific community take notice. Over a period of five years, from 1993 to 1998, they received, and recorded on film and camera, approximately eighty apportations and apparitions of angelic forms. They were happy to allow scrutiny and took their sessions to international locations for scientific validation. Overwhelming feelings of love were reported by the researchers. The most predominant message was: "It's love that matters most."

———— ✺ ————

"The way of truth and love has always won."

**—Mahatma Gandhi, lawyer and
civil rights leader, b. 1869**

CHAPTER 2

THE SECOND COMING: HAS IT ALREADY HAPPENED?

"For any speculation which does not at first look crazy, there is no hope."

—Freeman Dyson, physicist and author, b. 1923

"The universe is not only queerer than we suppose, but queerer than we can suppose."

—J. B. S. Haldane, scientist and innovator, b. 1892

COUNTLESS THOUSANDS OF books have been written about Jesus. He has been studied and debated for over two thousand years. He is the subject of millions of artworks. Same with music. Jesus is an influential and controversial figure who has had an enormous impact on our world. We are all touched by him, and will be touched by his second coming sooner or later.

The second coming is an auspicious, weighty topic, with weighty questions. Like ... Why is it important? How long have we been looking for it? How do we recognize it? Could it have already happened?

Importance of the Second Coming

Billy Graham, the late American evangelist who became one of the most influential Christian leaders of the twentieth century, wrote in the foreword to John Wesley White's book *Re-entry*:

> Probably no gospel theme apart from "Ye must be born again" is more relevant today, and I preach on some facet of this subject in virtually all of my crusades. Our world is filled with fear, hate, lust, greed, war and utter despair. Surely the second coming of Jesus Christ ... is the only hope of replacing these depressing features with trust, love, universal peace and prosperity. For it the world wittingly or inadvertently waits.

Can there be any doubt about the importance of the topic of the second coming? In that event lies the hope of millions of faithful Christians. Hope that everything that is wrong will finally be set right, either by some human agency or by God. It is how the second coming will be accomplished that is the big question.

John Wesley White was an associate evangelist with Billy Graham. In his book *Re-entry*, he drew parallels between New Testament signs and prophecies of Christ's return with actual current events of his day—the early 1970s. This is a practice that is still in wide use today—almost fifty years later. He wrote: "Man simply must have hope: future hope. That is why Bible prophecy in general and specifically the second coming of Christ is so relevant to the human situation today. Prophecy, that is, predictions of future events, occupies approximately one quarter of all Scripture."

What he wrote next is shocking: "The teaching of the second coming of our Lord is dealt with some 1,845 times in the Bible, 318 of these being in the New Testament. The return of the Lord is the dominant theme of 17 Old Testament books and one epistle in the New." (White, 1975:16)

White's next statement illustrates the importance of the topic. "In fact," states White, "7 out of every 10 chapters in the New Testament make reference to the second coming. Whole passages of the last half of the Bible are given over exclusively to its discussion."

If the second coming is dealt with 1,845 times in the Bible, and only 318 of these are in the New Testament, that leaves over fifteen hundred references to the second coming in the *Old* Testament. How could there be *any* reference to Jesus' coming again when he had not even come the *first* time? The prophecies in the Old Testament weren't enough to convince most Hebrews that the *first* coming of the Messiah had occurred. They are still waiting.

Jesus himself seemed to recognize that more than the fulfillment of Old Testament prophecies was needed to convince mankind of his Messiahship, according to John 17:21: "that they may all be one. As you, Father, are in me, and I am in you, may they also be in us, so that the world may believe that you have sent me."

Jesus was not recognized by most of his own people. The prophets of the Old Testament, with their apocalyptic writings, led the people to believe the Messiah would be a warrior with a sword come to smite their enemies. Even Jesus' own disciples thought he was a "fighting Messiah." But Jesus never condoned violence of any kind. He used every argument in his power to discourage the apocalyptic thinking of his day. His teachings did not promote death and destruction, but reconciliation and life. John 3:17 says: "God did not send the Son into the world to condemn the world, but in order that the world might be saved through him."

Robert Jewett, Professor of New Testament Interpretation at Garrett-Evangelical Theological Seminary, in *Jesus Against the Rapture: Seven Unexpected Prophecies,* reveals that it seems to be a well-kept secret among apocalyptic thinkers that Jesus' true attitude was that apocalyptic warfare should be avoided. He did not support the zealots who, by citing the same Old Testament prophecies we are hearing today, were promoting a climactic war with Rome. (Jewett, 1979: 11-12)

Timing of the Second Coming

When asked for a "sign of the times" Jesus' answer was: "No sign will be given … except the sign of Jonah." (Matt 16:4) Jonah wanted the destruction of Nineveh, but God acted with compassion instead. Isn't Jesus implying that it is God's will that the world be spared from the apocalyptic visioning of end-of-the-world thinkers?

In Luke 17:20, Jesus replied to the request for timing: "The Kingdom of God is not coming with things that can be observed." This is repeated in the "Little Apocalypse" of Mark: "But about that day or hour no one knows, neither the angels in heaven, nor the Son, but only the Father." (Mark 13:32) Even Jesus did not know when the end would occur. Nor did the angels. How could apocalyptic thinkers know?

Jesus warned about the consequences "for yourselves and for your children" if war was undertaken against Rome (Luke 23:28-31). In Luke 19:41-42, Jesus cried out: "If you… had only recognized on this day the things that make for peace!" The first-century zealots ignored Jesus' message and pushed their nation into a disastrous war. Destruction came to Jerusalem and their precious temple.

Sincere believers still reject the essential message of the historical Jesus they claim to serve. Either unaware or ignorant of the pacifistic overtones in Jesus' message, they become victims of the kind of prophecies about the "end times" that have brought disaster in the past, repeatedly.

On close examination, I could find no basis for John White's statement about the second coming references in the Old Testament. In the ones I checked, they seem to refer to prophecies about the *first* coming of a long-expected Messiah.

Clouds of Heaven

Take the following example from Daniel 7:13-14: "As I watched in the night visions, I saw one like a human being coming with the clouds of heaven. And he came to the Ancient One and was presented before him. To him was given dominion and glory and kingship ... that shall never be destroyed."

Note that this passage says "with the clouds *of heaven*"—*celestial* clouds, not terrestrial clouds. This is an important distinction.

The fulfillment of verse 13 could be the transfiguration on the mountain where Moses and Elijah (a.k.a. the Ancient One) appeared: "And there appeared to them Elijah with Moses, who were talking with Jesus.... Then a cloud overshadowed them, and from the cloud there came a voice, 'This is my Son, the Beloved; listen to him!'" (Mark 9:4-8)

The fulfillment of verse 14 could be demonstrated in Luke 23:40-43 when Jesus tells the malefactor on the cross next to his: "Today shalt thou be with me in paradise."

Today. *Not* after his second coming.

Many Christians are taught to believe that all that is necessary for salvation is acceptance of Jesus being their savior and dying on the cross for their sins. They believe that at death they will lie dormant in their graves until the advent of the second coming. But if the malefactor on the cross did not have to lie dormant in his grave, why would the rest of us?

The Second Birth

This view also does not consider what Jesus said to Nicodemas in John 3:3ff: "Very truly, I tell you, no one can see the kingdom of God without being born from above…. no one can enter the kingdom of God without being born of water and Spirit."

Hermes Trismegistus, sage of the second century A.D., referred to the importance of the second birth in "A Secret Discourse of Hermes Trismegistus to his son Tat, concerning Rebirth":

> He that is born by that birth is another … being wholly composed of Powers of God…. This sort of thing cannot be taught, my son; but God, when he so wills, recalls it to our memory…. it is not possible for you to see it with your organs of sight, which are fashioned out of material elements…. I am not now the man I was; I have been born again… To such eyes as yours, my son, I am not now visible. (p 241)

Let's look at another example from White's book, *Re-Entry*. (White, 1975: 20) He quotes Jesus from John 14:1-4:

> Set your troubled hearts at rest. Trust in God always; trust also in me. There are many dwelling-places in my Father's house; if it were not so I should have told you; for I am going there on purpose to prepare a place for you. And if I go and prepare a place for you, I shall come again and receive you to myself, so

that where I am you may be also; and my way there is known to you.

He then goes on to recite Thomas' question to Jesus, "Lord, we do not know where you are going, so how can we know the way?" (John 14:5) White then says: "Jesus replies with the familiar words which, obviously, apply to his coming again: 'I am the way; I am the truth and I am life: no one comes to the Father except by me' (John 14:6 NEB)."

White says it is obvious that these words by Jesus apply to his second coming. That is his interpretation. We will see later in this book what Jesus himself has to say about those words.

First, we must realize that the statement by Jesus "I am the way, the truth and the life," stated in the *present* tense, was about his *first* coming. White seems to be stretching it to mean that the *physical* presence of Jesus is necessary at some point in the future for man to get to heaven.

I assert that what Jesus meant was that by following his example of attaining at-one-ment with God, we too could have a similar relationship with God. Why else would Jesus have said: "the one who believes in me will also do the works that I do and, in fact, will do greater works than these, because I am going to the Father." (John 14:12)

Apocalypse Now?

"There is a kind of apocalyptic inoculation at work among these writers," states Jewett, "leading them to cite the authentic sayings of Jesus, but leaving them immune to their original meaning." They stay on the safe side, he says "by acknowledging that the precise date of the end is unknown, while insisting on an apocalyptic program of annihilation utterly alien to the Abba whom Jesus proclaimed." (Jewett, 1979: 23)

Jewett brings up a good question. Does God's nature change as the "end times" draw near? Jesus taught about a *loving* God. Are we to believe that His mercy wears thin because our modern-day sins are so great, and that He is suddenly going to lose patience with us and destroy it all? Many faithful Christians believe so.

I don't. If one has experienced the grace, mercy, compassion and Love of God, one cannot possibly think so.

In Mark 13:33-37, Jesus says: "Beware, keep alert; for you do not know when the time will come.... And what I say to you I say to all: Keep awake!"

Keep awake. No one knows when. Prepare for the unexpected.

As Huston Smith so eloquently points out in *Forgotten Truth*, modern science has taught us that the human imagination cannot comprehend things very large or very small:

> In those never-never, through-the-looking-glass abodes, parallel lines meet, curves get you from star to star more quickly than do Euclid's straight lines, a particle will pass through alternative apertures simultaneously without dividing, time shrinks and expands, [and] electrons (taking their cue from St. Thomas's angels who simply will themselves into different locations and find themselves there) jump orbit without traversing the intervening distance.... One might put the matter this way: If modern science showed that our senses are false witnesses, postmodern science is showing that the human imagination is comparably defective. (Smith, 1976: 105)

So how could we even begin to imagine the details of such a grandiose event as the second coming of Jesus? Or predict what it would be like until it actually happened? Newton believed God to be a Master Magician. I, too, believe God is the Master Magician of the Universe who, with His invisible sleight of hand, played a trick on all the fanatical cults and Doomsday Christians looking for the second coming of Jesus to be "in the clouds"—the *terrestrial* clouds, that is.

The Secret Second Coming

Wouldn't it be fitting of God's nature to manifest the second coming *secretly*, discreetly, and *non-violently*, right under the noses of those Armageddon Christians and cultists?

Hermes Trismegistus in *A Holy Book of Hermes Trismegistus Addressed to Asclepius* makes a relevant point on the importance of secrecy in revelation:

> You may call Ammon; but summon no one else, lest a discourse which treats of the loftiest of themes, and breathes the deepest reverence, should be profaned by the entrance and presence of a throng of listeners. For it would be impiety to make public through the presence of many witnesses a discussion which is replete with God in all his majesty. (Trismegistus, 2010: Prologue)

This auspicious event took place, secretly, in a way that no mortal has ever conceived of—through the automatic writing mediumship of James Padgett. Jesus even fulfilled the prophecy of his coming in the clouds, with hosts of angels, in these writings.

In drawings and cartoons, we symbolize people's thoughts with something like this:

Clouds. And when Jesus delivered these messages through Padgett, there were hosts of angels present.

"I am here to tell you that you had a cloud of witnesses as to your being selected to do my work, and you have wondered why so many of my disciples and apostles and those called saints should come to you in such close succession, and all testify as to that one fact. Well, I caused them to come as I wished to establish your faith as to my being the true Jesus of the Bible, and as to your mission in regard to my work."

—Jesus

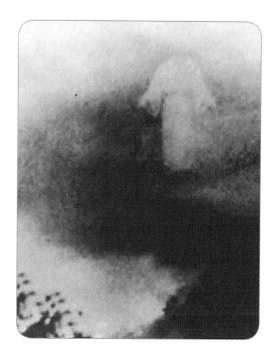

Jesus in the Clouds

Bill Sheehan testified that he took this photo from an airplane over Dallas, Texas, in 1961, and that he has the original negative. He claims everyone on the airplane saw it, and that three people with cameras took pictures. (https://www. youtube.com/watch?v=6V2w68mgORk)

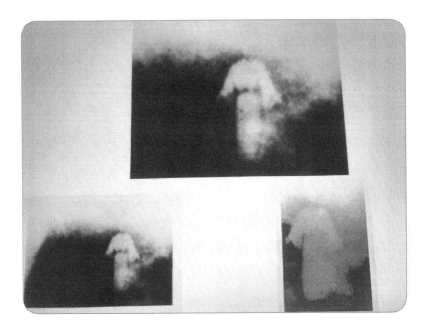

Pictures of Jesus in the clouds, purportedly taken with a Polaroid camera
(https://www.bibleprobe.com/jesusinclouds.htm)

CHAPTER 3

THE MOMENTOUS PADGETT MESSAGES

"Some regions of nature we experience directly, others we do not. But even these hidden regions can get messages to us in round-about ways or we would not know that they exist."

—Huston Smith, religious scholar and author, b. 1919

"So much is dependent upon the world getting the truths at this time, for men's souls are longing for the truth, and are [more] susceptible to receiving the same than ever in the history of mankind."

—Jesus of Nazareth, son of God and man, b. ~0

IT IS A remarkable fact that Jesus was a spiritualist. He exorcised demons and spirits—a *real* ghostbuster. He received the Spirit of God at his baptism by John (Matt 3:16). And he spoke with spirits, like Moses and Elijah in the transfiguration on the mountain in the gospels (Matt 17:1-9, Mark 9:2-8 and Luke 9:28-36). He appeared to many after his death (1Cor 15:8), and prophets in the early Christian communities stated words believed to be from the spirit of Jesus, Jesus Christ, or John.

The question here is: *What if there are contemporary writings from the living spirit of Jesus himself?* What if the material that's in the New Testament, which is about seventeen hundred years old, could be updated and viewed with greater clarity and understanding? What if there were answers to questions like: What was Jesus' childhood like? Did he ever regard himself to be God? Did his earthly body dematerialize at the resurrection, and, if so, by what means? Will Jesus ever return in the apocalyptic fashion expected by the early Christians and still believed by many Christians today?

The answers to all of these questions, and many more, are contained, in specific detail, in automatic writings claiming to be from Jesus through the mediumship of James E. Padgett at the beginning of the twentieth century.

The Momentous Padgett Messages

James Edward Padgett, born August 25, 1852, was not a cult leader or follower. He was an orthodox Methodist, and taught Sunday school for many years at the Trinity Methodist Church in Washington D.C. By profession, he was an attorney in Washington D.C. for forty-three years until his death in 1923. Padgett never received any money for his mediumship. He did not strive for or receive any notoriety.

Padgett's mediumship developed at the age of sixty-two under unique circumstances. In fact, he did not even believe in mediumship, but when his wife Helen died in February of 1914, his grief, coupled with a continuing experience of her presence, led him to attend a séance. The medium, Mrs. Maltby, told Padgett that he had the rare ability to receive automatic writings from spirits, and that his wife, Helen, wanted to write to him. She encouraged him to try on his own to receive communications. On his first attempt, the pencil moved automatically, but only produced what he called "fish hooks" and "hangers."

After many tries, he finally discovered a short, personal message on the paper, signed by Helen. It stated that she was often with him and happy that she was able to communicate with him. Still, he questioned the source of these writings and demanded more proof. The writings that followed told of personal events in their lives that *only* the two of them could have known.

Padgett felt that this information could be coming from thoughts originating in his own mind. But the writings were more rapid than his own thought processes, and the author kept insisting that it was *not* his own mind but hers relaying the messages. Helen repeatedly wrote of her love for him and how happy it made her to be with him. And she wrote about the automatic writing happening through him: "You do not do the thinking but merely let the thoughts pass through your brain, and the movement of the pencil is caused by the exercise of your brain in conjunction with my power which I exercise on the pencil.... you do not originate the thought but merely convey it to the hand which I guide in accordance with my thought." (Padgett, 1958: II:14)

She further explained that he does not have anything more to do with what is written "than an electric wire has to do with transmitting a message from the party at the end where the message is given." She clarified it another way: "When I think a thought I pass it through your brain to your hand and my power to move your hand is brought into action, just as when you think a thought your power to move your hand is brought into action."

Repetition is a virtue in these messages, so Helen affirms it again: "My thoughts are not your thoughts; and when I think, your mind catches the thought but does not create the same. So, you must believe that I am doing the writing and not you—for I write some thoughts which you could not write if you tried. How do you like that for assurance?" (Padgett, 1958: II:14)

This phenomenon is commonly called automatic writing in the United States. It should not be confused with what Brazilian Spiritists call automatic writing, which is no more than the manifestation of one's subconscious. What was happening here to Padgett is called *psicografica* in Brazil, a manifestation coming from a separate entity, presumably a spirit.

Spirit Communication and Progression

Padgett, intrigued and perplexed by these events, began a serious study of spiritualism. So much of the information he received differed from his orthodox Christian views and portrayed an afterlife in a spirit world where one continued to learn and progress through various realms. He also learned that, if given the chance and under the right circumstances, spirit-to-mortal communication could occur.

He asked his wife what plane or sphere she was in. Helen wrote that she was in a plane of the second sphere where there was a degree of happiness and light, and that her ability to visit him and write by controlling his brain and hand was "quite easy." As a result, she wasn't interested in attempting to progress to higher spheres. Padgett told his close friend, Dr. Leslie R. Stone, that he could feel her presence intensely at these times and that it made him feel a happiness that was alien to him except when she wrote. (Padgett, 1958: I:vi)

In his spiritual studies, Padgett had discovered that a spirit could progress to greater happiness and higher spheres, and he encouraged Helen to do this. She did, with the help of Padgett's grandmother, Ann Rollins, who was later described by Helen as "a glorious spirit dwelling in the high Celestial heavens." Ann told her that to progress to these higher Celestial realms one must "pray to the heavenly Father for His Love through earnest longing of soul."

These sessions, at first held to receive writings from Helen, had become infused with a deep spirituality, replacing much of the personal material. Helen prayed as instructed. Her prayers were soon answered, and as this Divine Love of God entered her soul, she experienced her thoughts and desires becoming purified. This, in turn, became reflected through a changed soul, causing her spirit body to become brighter and more ethereal. Helen had reached the third sphere, she later wrote, and was considerably happier.

Transformation

Helen suggested that Padgett and his four friends who were witnesses to these sessions (Dr. Leslie R. Stone, Eugene Morgan, Dr. Goerger, and Rollison Colburn) should also pray for God's Love since "the soul is the same, whether in the flesh or spirit body, [and] it could be transformed by prayer to the Father for His Divine Love. Not by ordinary intellectual prayers that come from the head, but from the heart and soul." (Padgett, 1958: I:vii)

Padgett at first couldn't believe this. But later writings informed him that he should not doubt and that Jesus himself, still interested in helping humanity, would write through him of this sacred truth, if he would allow him to.

Though this did eventually happen, he felt that it was absurd to believe Jesus had written, and Padgett destroyed the first message he received signed "Jesus of the Bible." One of the four witnesses, Rollison Colburn, was skeptical to the point of leaving the group.

But Goerger, Morgan and Stone shared an intuitive sense that the message was genuine. On September 28, 1914, Jesus delivered his first formal message through Padgett—a long message which urged him to pray for God's Love, and stated that certain passages in the New Testament, completely believed by Padgett, were false. The full message is in the Appendix.

He was still full of doubt and conflict. Many of the ideas about soul progression, Jesus *not* being conceived by the Holy Spirit, and other falsehoods in the Bible, went *against* what he learned and what he was teaching in Sunday school. Yet, in reflecting on this and discussing it with his close friend, Dr. Stone, he finally came to the realization that, this being the case, there was no way these differing ideas could have come from his own mind. All these spirits, including Jesus, must be who they said they were. Dr. Stone wrote that it was at this point that Padgett and his friends began to pray as instructed:

> …letting our soul longings go out to the Heavenly Father, and in time a feeling came glowing involuntarily into the region of our hearts. We felt this emotion grow stronger and stronger with continued fervid prayers and as we did so, our faith in God became solidified and absolute. Never before had he, nor I, felt so sure of the real existence of the Father and His Divine Love and mercy. The cold intellectual concept which we had entertained of Him had through prayers for His Love been transformed into a warm, glowing, living feeling of closeness, of at-onement with the Heavenly Father, whose Love and

mercy and goodness we could sense were personal and real. (Padgett, 1958: I:ix)

If you desire, you can read Dr. Leslie R. Stone's entire testimony at http://secondnewtestament.org/stonetestimony.html.

Requirements for Celestial Mediumship

According to Jesus, two things are necessary for an authentic medium to receive messages about God's truths. First, the medium must have complete faith that the Celestial spirits are real beings who can control the brain and hand if the soul is in the right condition. The Celestials could not make contact if the medium did not have this faith. Second, the medium had to follow instructions and pray to God for Divine Love, in a willing submission to the conditions imposed by the spirits. Only God's Love had the power to transform the medium's brain so it could accommodate the thoughts of the high Celestial spirits. This brain transformation is only accomplished through the development of the soul.

Padgett continued to follow the advice of ongoing messages from Helen, from Ann Rollins, and, above all, from Jesus, encouraging him to keep praying for God's Love so that he could receive messages of religious importance for humanity from the highest Celestial spirits, including Jesus and his apostles. This progression in Divine Love was necessary to change the condition of Padgett's soul to more closely match that of the Celestial spirits. In doing so, his brain would change enough to enable it to receive, and his hand to automatically write, the thoughts that they desired to impart about God, Jesus' mission, the New Testament and Christianity.

The following message from John, the disciple of Jesus, explained the conditions: "We must have a mind that is filled with thoughts of the higher things of truth, even though we do not use those thoughts. Our thoughts are all spiritual, and our truths can be received only by the mind in a spiritual condition." John clarified: "And when I say mind I merely mean the organs of the brain as influenced by the thoughts of the mind; for I will tell you what you may not know, that these component organs of the brain are not always and under all conditions receptive of the same control by the minds of spirits." (Padgett, 1958: II:218)

John wrote that one can receive a long and profound message through the brain about material things, yet "under similar conditions of these organs, not be able to receive messages of the higher truths." (Padgett, 1958: II:218) The condition of the brain is caused by the spiritual condition of the soul.

"A medium who is merely intellectual and morally good cannot receive those messages of the higher truths," wrote John, "because there can be no rapport between the brain of such a medium and the mind of the higher spirit who may desire to communicate." (Padgett, 1958: II:218-219) This is why messages from earth-bound spirits or from those who have only intellectual development are so often received by mediums instead of messages from spirits with high soul development.

The following statement in a letter from Jesus tried to reassure Padgett about the source of the material coming through his hand: "What you have written [are] my thoughts—you did not think any of these thoughts." (Padgett, 1958: I:24) And he made it clear to Padgett what was at stake: "There are many messages to be written and I am anxious that you receive them in order that they may be delivered to the world, for the world is now awakening to a greater realization of the fact that man is spiritual and must have spiritual food." (Padgett, 1958: III:206)

Why Padgett?

Jesus told Padgett he was not selected because he was less sinful than other men or that he was the best medium that had ever lived. It was because he had been willing to believe that Jesus could actually come to him and he was willing to ask for, and open to receiving, the Divine Love. Jesus reveals:

> There are certain qualities in your constitution, both spiritual and material, that render you susceptible to the influences of our powers and to the use by us for the purpose of our design and work, which determines one to choose you for the work in the way in which I and the other high spirits have heretofore used you; and it may seem strange to you that in all the long ages preceding, I have not found one human with the qualification to fit him for the work. (Padgett, 1958: I:3-4)

Jesus said he tried to use others before, but they failed to submit their minds, souls, beliefs and forethoughts to his influence and instructions. Many humans have the qualifying conditions of spiritual and material makeup, but they also have free wills, which cannot be compelled. Circumstances, environments, education and beliefs are all elements that affect and determine the possibility of finding a suitable medium. Jesus writes:

> All things in the spirit world, as well as on earth, are controlled by immutable laws, and all spirits as well as mortals are subject to those laws. The law of rapport and communication must be complied with by spirits, no matter how much elevated, and also by humans; and no spirit, by reason of the possession of any supposed power, can set aside this law. But while spirits

have not this power, yet they may have such knowledge of conditions that they can discern what qualities in the condition of a human are susceptible to the influence, and molding by the spirits, so that as a result thereof, the law may be brought into operation. (Padgett, 1958: I:3-4)

Jesus explained that he had been working for a long time to influence Padgett's mind and beliefs, so his soul could become developed for the rapport that would permit the Celestials to transmit their messages.

Proof of Jesus

How do we know it was really Jesus? First, if the "Jesus" writing through Padgett wasn't the real Jesus of Nazareth, but some spirit claiming to be him, it would be a spirit with evil intentions. But in the writings, Padgett was often encouraged to go to spirit-filled churches for spiritual food. A spirit with evil intentions would not have suggested that.

Second, Padgett received assurances in letters from Andrew and John that no spirit would be allowed to impersonate Jesus or any of his disciples. If any spirits tried, the high spirits would compel them to stop and leave Padgett alone. "Nothing but the truth will be written," John stated, "and further, we will not allow any spirit who is not in our band, or who has not this Divine Love to write on any of the truths that are necessary to be revealed to the world." (Padgett, 1958: I:339)

Third, the communications from Jesus sound like him. The following letter from Jesus asserted:

You are my friend and disciple. You are in me and I am in thee, and we are in the Father. You are in me for all eternity. My

kingdom is not of this world and you are not of this world—
you are in me as I told my disciples of old. Only believe me
and keep my commandments, and I will love you to the end,
and the Father will love you. (Padgett, 1958: II:23)

That sounds like the same Jesus in John 17:21: "that they may all
be one. As you, Father, are in me and I am in you, may they also be in
us, so that the world may believe that you have sent me... and have
loved them even as you have loved me."

Jesus' disciples also wrote through Padgett to corroborate, inform,
and reassure him of the source of his automatic writings:

I am the true Andrew of the Bible, and no other, and you
must believe that I am. I know that you may have doubts as
to so many of the disciples of the Master coming to you to
write, but you must not be surprised at that fact, for who are
more interested in the great work that you are to do than the
disciples of the Master, who know that his teachings are the
truth, and that mankind needs them at this time, more than at
any time in the history of the world. (Padgett, 1958: II:96-97)

Importance of Love

A letter from James, apostle of Jesus, states the importance of God's
Love, Divine Love, as the way to the *true* New Birth and blissful
immortality. He reveals that no founder of any race or sect has ever
taught the inflowing of the Divine Love in contradistinction to that
of the natural love. The teachings of Jesus are the only ones that reveal
the existence of this Divine Love. James writes: "The teachings of the
other founders will show men the way to a life of happiness, and to
what they may suppose is continuous existence. But the teachings of

Jesus are the only ones that declare and lead men to a realization of the true immortality of the soul." (Padgett, 1958: I:158)

The importance of love is eloquently expressed by the Apostle Paul, who was knocked off his horse and slain in the spirit by his encounter with the resurrected Jesus when Paul (then Saul) was on his way to Damascus to persecute Christians. This experience transformed him into Christianity's greatest evangelist. In the first letter to the Corinthians, Paul expounds on the highest gift of all, love: "If I speak in the tongues of mortals and of angels, but do not have love, I am a noisy gong or a clanging cymbal. And if I have prophetic powers, and understand all mysteries and all knowledge, and if I have all faith, so as to remove mountains, but do not have love, I am nothing." (1 Cor 13:1-3)

A few verses later, Paul makes a powerful statement on the indestructible nature of love, even as prophecies and knowledge undergo change and obsolescence:

> Love never ends. But as for prophecies, they will come to an end; as for tongues, they will cease; as for knowledge, it will come to an end. For we know only in part, and we prophesy only in part; but when the complete comes, the partial will come to an end. When I was a child, I spoke like a child, I thought like a child, I reasoned like a child; when I became an adult, I put an end to childish ways. For now we see in a mirror, dimly, but then we will see face to face. Now I know only in part; then I will know fully, even as I have been fully known. And now faith, hope, and love abide, these three; and the greatest of these is love. (1 Cor 13:8-13)

In his letter to the Romans, Paul expresses the conviction that nothing can separate us from God's Love: "For I am convinced that neither death, nor life, nor angels, nor rulers, nor things present, nor things to come, nor powers, nor height, nor depth, nor anything else in all creation, will be able to separate us from the love of God in Christ Jesus." (Romans 8:38-39)

———➤✦←———

The answers to many questions about the authenticity of these unprecedented messages are within Padgett's story and within the messages themselves. But we must put any religious or spiritual revelation through a crucible of discernment. The following chapters explore more evidence and issues related to authority, especially in comparison with the apostolic origin of the New Testament writings. The New Testament is examined through the lenses of modern Biblical criticism, including form, source, textual, historical, and redaction criticism. We also look at issues surrounding the formation of the New Testament canon, like grappling with continuing revelation.

But first we step even further back, into Old Testament times, to discover the origins of resistance to communication with deceased spirits.

———➤✦←———

CHAPTER 4

REVELATION: PROPHECY, SPIRITUALISM, AND OLD TESTAMENT INFLUENCES

"Now if people say to you, 'Consult the ghosts and the familiar spirits that chirp and mutter; should not a people consult their gods, the dead on behalf of the living, for teaching and for instruction?' Surely, those who speak like this will have no dawn... They will... see only distress and darkness, the gloom of anguish; and they will be thrust into thick darkness." (Isaiah 8:19-20, 22)

"When you come into the land that the Lord your God is giving you, you must not learn to imitate the abhorrent practices of those nations. No one shall be found among you who... practices divination, or is a soothsayer, or

an augur, or a sorcerer, or one who casts spells, or who consults ghosts or spirits, or who seeks oracles from the dead." (Deuteronomy 18: 9-11)

VAST NUMBERS OF contemporary Christians have adopted a negative view of spiritualism, arising from Old Testament sources like the ones cited above. Especially Fundamentalist Christians, who proclaim that the Bible is the "infallible Word of God." They quote passages like those above to suggest that a faithful Christian would never engage in mediumship or spiritualism.

Yet there are examples in the Old Testament of unsolicited positive experiences with spirits. And examination of the Old Testament tradition shows that the prophets, and the patriarchs who preceded them, came from outside the status quo and were channels of information from higher spiritual realms or from God. They were mediums.

This contradiction in the Old Testament raises some questions:

- What is the origin of the adversity to mediumship in the Israelite faith, and, hence, in the Christian faith?
- What are the similarities and differences between prophecy and spiritualism?
- How do you discern between a false prophet and a true prophet?
- What are common characteristics of true prophets?
- What is the nature of divine revelation?

Roots of Exclusivity

Let's consider the origins of the ancient Yahwist ban on the "cult of the dead." Yahwist refers to a writer (or writers) of one of the earliest sources of the Torah, the first five books of the Old Testament, in which God is called Yahweh. According to Norman Gottwald, Professor Emeritus of Biblical Studies at New York Theological Seminary and author of *The Tribes of Yahweh*, the major developments in social organization and religious ideology for the Ancient Israelites took place during the inter-tribal period, by the mid-eleventh century B.C.

Gottwald describes the Mono-Yahwism of the early Israelite tribes. Common elements included sanctions *against* religious mystifications like ancestor worship and speculation about life after death: "The dead were dead and were not to be lavishly memorialized, worshipped, or communicated with." They acknowledged death, but took away the "magico-religious potency which [it] often had in other Near Eastern religions." (Gottwald, 1979: 614-615)

It was not until late in the post-exilic age, after Alexander the Great, that the Israelites began to acquire any hope of an afterlife. Then, because of the persecution and martyrdom suffered during the exile, they began to question whether life continued after death. Intermarriage with pagans and the beliefs of neighboring nations also influenced them to include a belief in the afterlife. The idea of the individual as an entity, as opposed to just part of a clan or nation, was also uncommon before this time.

The Books of Ezra and Nehemiah show that by the fifth century B.C. the Israelites were losing their special sense of identity as a covenant people. They slowly drifted into pagan marriages that cost many their faith, a faith that had given them a special identity, with great emphasis on the election of Israel as a chosen people by Yahweh, the One and Only God. They felt a need to be holy, and separate, as a community, to give witness to other nations.

This extremely nationalistic stance did not allow for foreign influences. They were not to intermarry because of the fear that it would dilute or negate their faith and they would take steps backward, not forward, in their knowledge of God.

The first time we see an expression of a belief in resurrection of the dead, and judgment at death, in the Old Testament is in the Book of Daniel. This idea originally came from the Persian prophet Zoroaster. Before this time, during all but the last two hundred years of the Old Testament period, for more than eighteen hundred years, the Ancient Israelites thought death to be *totally final*.

Their worldview included no joy after death. They thought the grave was a pit or swamp, where a person returned to the dust of the earth. (Psalm 16:10; Job 34:14-15; Boadt, 1984) Death was destruction and emptiness. No God. No singing praises.

Sheol, the dwelling of the dead, was believed to be a place of stillness, darkness, and total helplessness where the spirit resided after the grave had taken the body. It was a place of no power and no hope, with bodies lying row on row. (Isaiah 14:10; Ezekiel 32:17-31; Boadt, 1984) In Jewish thought, the soul or spirit was connected to the body, not separate.

This was *not* the thinking of the other nations in their region. The Greeks believed the spirit dwelled in the body, and when the body died, the spirit went to the spirit world. In Egypt, the dead were thought to live on in much the same way they had in life. Their belief in a blessed afterlife was highly developed.

Converted by Zoroaster in the early sixth century B.C., Persian belief included good and evil spirits. And angels, most of whom were assistants of the One God who was lord of all, Ahura Mazda. Zoroaster also introduced the concept of a moral judgment at death determining one's placement in either heaven, with its eternal reward in a paradise of all good things, or hell, described as a lake of fire. (Boadt, 1984)

Since the Ancient Israelites did not believe in any life after death, of what use would it be to communicate with the dead? There would be no power in it, no hope. Only darkness, helplessness, and emptiness.

There are some notable exceptions to this almost complete rejection of the spirit world. One exception is that the Ancient Israelites often explained illnesses without any clear external physical cause, like the plague or pneumonia, by accusing evil spirits of creating the sickness. The Old Testament also suggests a belief that associated evil spirits with human suffering. Psalm 91 talks of pestilence stalking victims. Leviticus 16 talks about the demon Azazel, to whom Aaron makes an offering each year as atonement for the sins of Israel. No one would want to communicate with these evil spirits.

There are also examples in the Old Testament of people interacting with higher spiritual entities, especially angels. The story of Jacob's ladder in Genesis 28:12-13 illustrates a dream where angels are ascending and descending on a ladder from heaven.

Another important example is the angel in Genesis 22:11-19 who comes to save Abraham's beloved son Isaac from sacrifice. Balaam (Numbers 22:23-36) and Hagar (Genesis 16:7-15) also encountered angels with important messages. And, in 1 Samuel 28:6-20, Saul, in desperation because the spirit of God had left him, calls Samuel from the dead through the medium of Endor, even after banishing all the mediums in his own nation.

Samuel and Saul both wrote messages through Padgett about the medium of Endor. She was not a witch and did not practice the black arts. She was a good woman, of good moral character, who possessed powers to "call up the dead," as they were called. She did not cast spells or use charms, but was a true medium, having around her "many spirits of the higher order whose only desires were to do good to mortals." (Padgett, 1958: I:268) She was, wrote Samuel, "careful to have no evil spirits come and communicate, and her powers with the higher ones were very great. Had she been of what you call the lower class of mediums, I would never have responded to her call." (Padgett, 1958: I:268)

Samuel points out that it was only natural that Saul would come to him for guidance after he became a spirit since he had instructed and advised Saul when alive. Mediums were numerous in those days, "and because of their being so common and of such different kinds, and the most of them engaged in necromancy and evil arts, there were passed strict laws against them pursuing their calling or engaging in the practice of consulting spirits." (Padgett, 1958: I:268) Many of them were not bad, but did good in the world, "and among these was the woman of Endor, notwithstanding that she has been so vilified and abused by the churches and preachers. You may be surprised when I tell you that she is now living high up in the Celestial Heavens and a redeemed spirit enjoying the Divine Love of God." (Padgett, 1958: I:268-269) [The entire message from Saul is included in the Appendix.]

Gottwald says one reason for the ban on mediumship may have been a diametrical reaction against the Egyptian emphasis on the afterlife. A huge amount of communal resources went for the cult of the dead. The Egyptian preoccupation with ancestor worship and memorialization of the dead were exhausting, socially and economically.

The lavish expenditures made on the cult of the dead did not jeopardize the living standards of the ruling class. They continued to enjoy luxury and opulence. It actually allowed the ruling class to put a larger surplus of wealth, which came from the populace, into self-indulgent, squandered efforts to assure immortality. This made a negative impression on Moses' generation. "By renouncing the grip of the dead upon the living," states Gottwald, "Yahwism struck a blow at the ideological supports of stratified society and at the same time released the economic products for direct consumption by the living instead of wasting them in sacrifices and memorials to the dead." (Gottwald, 1979: 694)

Prophecy and Spiritualism

A close look at prophecy and examination of the Old Testament prophets reveal common characteristics. Ernest Sellin and George Fohrer, biblical scholars and authors of *Introduction to the Old Testament*, give an excellent definition of prophecy: "A prophet or prophetess is... consciously aware of having been singled out and called, who feels constrained to proclaim messages and perform actions suggested in the form of divine revelations during a state of spiritual inspiration, possibly accompanied by mild or intense ecstasy." (Sellin & Fohrer, 1968: 343)

Johannes Lindblom, scholar of Old Testament prophecy and author of *Prophecy in Ancient Israel* says it is typical of all prophetic personalities to feel that what they have to say "is given them from above, that they are only mouthpieces of another, speaking to them and through them." (Lindblom, 1962: 43)

Now consider the definition of medium in *Prophecy and Society in Ancient Israel* by Robert Wilson, Professor of Old Testament and Religious Studies at Yale Divinity School. He writes that the term "medium," often found in anthropological literature, is used "as a broad designation for anyone who acts as a channel of communication between the human and divine realms. People come to the medium to ask questions of the spirits, and the spirits, in turn, speak to the inquirers in a recognizable way through the medium." (Wilson, 1980: 25)

Wilson uses comparative anthropology to understand the social dimensions of prophetic activity. He states, "The prophet, shaman, medium, and diviner are all characterized by the fact that in some way they serve as intermediaries between the human and divine worlds." (Wilson, 1980: 25)

According to these definitions, the prophet and medium sound identical, but they are not. A prophet is a medium, but a medium is not necessarily a prophet. C.H. Dodd, British biblical scholar and author of *The Authority of the Bible* states: "The prophets, however one is to explain their experience, were distinctly conscious that a word came to them from beyond the limits of their conscious personality and brought them new truth—'thus spoke Jehovah'." (Dodd, 1929) New truth from God. Divine revelation. This is the territory of the prophets.

Israel did not have a monopoly on prophecy. Other cultures around them had prophets who were mouthpieces for God. In Numbers 22-24, the story of Balaam is an example of a foreign prophet being a mouthpiece for God. Even though paid by the king of Moab to curse Israel, only blessings came out because God put the words in Balaam's mouth. "The word God puts in my mouth, that is what I must say." (Numbers 22:38)

Archaeological proof that a seer named Balaam existed comes from an inscription found in the Transjordan, an area to the east of the Jordan River, dating about 700 B.C. The inscription reports sayings about the future made by Balaam, the seer.

Five letters from about 1700 B.C. from the great Babylonian city of Mari speak of the appearance of a "messenger of God" and of a "prophetess." Klaus Koch, Old Testament scholar and author of *The Prophets*, writes about this appearance of prophets in the Mari letters: "They belong to a class of men and women associated with the temple of a deity, from whom they received messages through omens, dreams, and ecstatic experiences; they pronounced these messages as oracles." (Koch, 1983: 344) In Babylonia, priests and priestesses supported the king by means of "spoken dreams." For Assyria, Koch says, there is evidence of "another kind of ecstatic prophecy through individual priestesses known by name, especially in the Ishtar temple of Arbela." (Koch, 1983: 344)

Prophetic phenomena are not isolated to one race, country, or religion. Prophets are everywhere in the world and at all stages of religious development. Lindblom states that even though it is true that ecstasy is contagious between individuals, it is not accurate to say that ecstasy or prophecy is borrowed by one people from another: "These phenomena have arisen in different regions quite independently. The prophetic endowment is deeply rooted in human nature; what may be borrowed from other quarters is the behaviour and the forms... the external manifestations." (Lindblom, 1962: 32)

Sellin & Fohrer talk about the stages of development of the prophetic oracle. The first stage consists of a moment when the prophet, transported to another sphere, experiences the "spirit" or "word" of God in a personal experience of God. In this moment, the prophet has a "secret experience," including visions like in Isaiah 6, auditions like in Jeremiah 4, and sudden inspirations like in Isaiah 7:

> The secret experience takes place in the full light of spiritual and intellectual consciousness but can be accompanied by an ecstatic experience.... the prophet is gripped by a power that he cannot escape. What he experiences or perceives he is constrained to put into words and to proclaim. (Jeremiah 20:9; Amos 3:8) Therefore, immediately after his secret experience the prophet begins to ponder over it. (Sellin, 1968: 349-350)

The second stage consists of the prophet's interpretation and exposition of his unique experience, according to his own faith. The experience is incorporated into the prophet's previous picture of God, enlarging and enlivening it. This interpretation, says Sellin and Fohrer, usually distinguishes between true and false prophecy. But from whose perspective?

Genuine or False Prophet

The problem of false prophecy, of knowing who among the various voices speaking for God was actually speaking the truth, became a very serious problem during Old Testament times. It is a problem that continues to this day. Both genuine and false prophets speak with authority, saying, "Thus says the Lord." Who are we to believe? What distinguishes a true prophet from a false prophet?

One proof, which Jeremiah used against Hananiah in Jeremiah 28, was that the words of a true prophet would eventually come to pass. 1 and 2 Kings contain many examples of this theme of prophets validated by the fulfillment of their prophecies. (Ahijah in 1 Kings 11-12 and 1 Kings 14-15; Jehu in 1 Kings 16; Micaiah ben Imiah in 1 Kings 22; Elijah in 2 Kings 1; Elisha in 2 Kings 7; and Hulda (a prophetess) in 2 Kings 11 and 23.)

The Deuteronomists used the same criteria for dealing with prophetic disputes: "If a prophet speaks in the name of the Lord but the thing does not take place or prove true, it is a word that the Lord has not spoken." (Deu 18:22)

But, this test is applied in retrospect, not when the prophecy is spoken. So, what happens when Jeremiah or Isaiah predict something that does not happen? Does that mean they are not true prophets? Are they allowed to be human as well as a divine mouthpiece for God?

What about the possibility of a false prophet who happens to predict something that comes true? Does that automatically make them a "Prophet of God"? Of course not. Perhaps they made an educated or lucky guess.

So, we cannot rely on the fulfillment of prophecy as proof of a true prophet.

A proof put forth in 1 Kings 18 was that the presence of Yahweh would be with the true prophet and absent from the false one. Yahweh was a *living* god, not a dead one like Baal, the king of the nature gods worshipped by the Canaanite cults. Elijah demonstrated this at Mt. Carmel when he challenged the prophets of Baal in a contest to the death, standing up against the pagan queen Jezebel who had been persecuting and killing the prophets of Yahweh. All the false pagan prophets were slain on the spot when Elijah proved Yahweh to be the living God and Baal to be absent.

1 Kings 19 reports that Elijah, like Moses, was granted a vision of God. He experienced a great wind, earthquake, and fire, but God was not in these events.

Then there was sheer silence and it is in this silence that God revealed Himself—in the voice of the Spirit heard by prophets, not in the powers of nature.

To find and know God, we must *not* look to nature. He is not found there. God wants us to know Him and go directly to Him in silent prayer and meditation—not be distracted by lower forms of His creation—when it comes to guidance about moral and spiritual development.

The worship of many gods who were little more than the personification of elements of nature would be empty and fruitless, like trying to know what a butterfly is like by looking at an anthill. According to the pre-exilic prophets Hosea and Isaiah, God abhorred such empty worship. "For I desire steadfast love and not sacrifice, the knowledge of God rather than burnt offerings." (Hosea 6:6)

Not much was known about the prophets until the middle of the eighth century B.C. when a breakthrough occurred in ancient Hebrew prophecy. Amos, and other writing prophets after him (Isaiah, Hosea, and Jeremiah), gave us the opportunity to study their actual words.

Before then we only had scanty stories about prophets, and these were often exaggerated into legends. Their backgrounds seem to be unimportant, except for their "anointing" or "call" (1 Kings 19:16).

This calling goes a long way in giving a prophet credibility. A vision also grants the prophetic status, as in 2 Kings 2:1-12 when Elisha sees Elijah ascend to heaven in a whirlwind. (See 1 Kings 22:19-22; Amos 7:1-9, 8:1-3; Zechariah 1:7-6:8; Daniel 7-12.)

The Call of God

The Call of God is what gives the prophets inspiration, drive, and energy to do the will of God. It gives them their spiritual purpose, their job. Indeed, the experience with God must have been so glorious and transforming (Moses "shines" after being with God) that it would inspire them to perform miracles, like Moses and Elijah, and withstand loneliness, persecution and the possibility of losing one's life, like Jeremiah. [See call reports in Exodus 3-6 (Moses); Isaiah 6; Jeremiah 1; Ezekiel 1-3.]

Gerhard von Rad, Professor of Old Testament at the University of Heidelberg, states in *The Message of the Prophets*:

> This was more than a new profession: it was a totally new way of life, even at the sociological level, to the extent that a call meant relinquishing normal social life and all the social and economic securities which this offered, and changing over instead to a condition where a man had nothing to depend upon, or, as we may put it, to a condition of dependence upon Yahweh and upon that security alone. (Von Rad, 1967: 37)

This new way of life meant completely surrendering to God—giving God control over your life and words, even if it meant having to wait a long time for an answer from God, and even if it meant endangering your life.

When Jeremiah went to the temple to give God's warnings, his words so angered the priests and temple prophets that they wanted him dead. He was immediately put on trial.

In his own defense, Jeremiah said he had acted on God's command. After all, would he have come of his own free choice to tell his own nation that God was going to wipe them out if they did not repent of their sins and surrender to the enemy? He knew it would be considered treason. The people and the royalty became convinced he was a prophet and spared him.

The idea of being "lifted up" into the heavens was the ultimate test of the true prophet for both Jeremiah (Jeremiah 23) and Micaiah (1 Kings 22). The prophet, lifted into a higher spiritual realm, becomes aware of a revelation which God intends to bring to the world in that particular time and context. It increases the faith of the people or contributes to what is known about God. Like when God revealed to Elijah that He comes in the voice of the Spirit given to prophets.

Revelation, by definition, is secret in nature, between God and His chosen prophet. "Surely the Lord God does nothing, without revealing his secret to his servants the prophets." (Amos 3:7)

The Presence of God

Gerhard von Rad was a German theologian who pioneered the "tradition history" approach to biblical studies. This method emphasizes the role of oral traditions in the formation of the Old Testament, and has dominated the study of the Bible. He discusses a common characteristic of the prophets—that the presence of the "spirit of Yahweh" was a part of their very constitution. In 2 Kings 2:9, Elisha requests Elijah for possession of it, and only after it had rested upon him is he considered a prophet. His associates attested to this presence of the "spirit of God," and this sanctioned him in their eyes. (Von Rad, 1967)

We have another example of the "spirit of God" coming upon Saul after his anointing as the first king of Israel: "Then the spirit of the Lord will possess you, and you will be in a prophetic frenzy along with them and be turned into a different person." (1 Sam 10:6) Von Rad writes:

> ...the prophets, in their new and completely unprecedented situation, were faced with the need to justify themselves both in their own and in other people's eyes. The event... forced him to justify his exceptional status in the eyes of the majority. This makes clear that the writing down of a call was something secondary to the call itself, and that it served a different end from the latter. The call commissioned the prophet: the act of writing down an account of it was aimed at those sections of the public in whose eyes he had to justify himself. (Von Rad, 1967: 34-5)

Von Rad further states that the importance the prophets attached to their call makes it quite clear that they felt apart from the religious status quo. Jeremiah used strong language against false prophets who claim to have visions or dreams, but only speak from their own minds or imaginations: "Thus says the Lord of hosts: Do not listen to the words of the prophets who prophesy to you; they are deluding you. They speak visions of their own minds, not from the mouth of the Lord... I did not speak to them, yet they prophesied." (Jeremiah 23:16, 21)

There is universal agreement that visions and auditions came to the prophets from outside themselves, and that they came suddenly and completely, without premeditation. (Von Rad, 1967) Authentic prophecy and mediumship must start outside oneself.

But, there are many influences outside one's self and all sorts of spirits with a wide range of development. Also affecting the *quality* of mediumship are one's motives, intentions, and deep inner longings.

> Say to those who prophesy out of their own imagination: "Hear the word of the Lord!" Thus says the Lord God, Alas for the senseless prophets who follow their own spirit, and have seen nothing!... They have envisioned falsehood and lying divination; they say, "Says the Lord," when the Lord has not sent them, and yet they wait for the fulfillment of their word! Have you not seen a false vision or uttered a lying divination, when you have said, "Says the Lord," even though I did not speak? (Ezekiel 13:2-4; 6-7) (See also Jeremiah 14:4)

Sometimes a person presents that he is imparting knowledge originating from an outside source, but it is only coming from his own imagination. There is usually a hidden motive or agenda that is self-motivated. Not God-motivated. Perhaps his desire is for self-aggrandizement, self-indulgence, or any number of other impure or sinful motives. These may include manipulating, controlling, and deceiving others.

Everyone is a channel or medium for something. We are all affected by outside forces. Which influences we listen to depend on factors like motivation, drive, education, experience, health, and social and cultural conventions. What is the medium a channel for? Why? How do you recognize "mental" mediumship, or lower spirit mediumship, especially when the medium is saying it is coming from God or an angel of God?

Discernment of Divine Revelation

We must always question what is being spoken and rely on our own soul perceptions in relationship with God. An intense, unwavering desire for truth is paramount. If questions or doubts come up, they should be allowed to kindle a bright flame of scrutiny in pursuit of what is true.

An untruth, either immediately or over time, will be perceived as the discord or disharmony that it is. Truth will prove itself. It will stand up under the light of intense scrutiny. It can be tossed, turned, and thrown every which way and still land upright. It will stand the test of time and join the chorus of universal harmony.

To know if a revelation is from God we must know and trust ourselves, and the Divine image in which we were created. We should go to the highest source, God, for the answers. "Among all the wise ones of the nations and in all their kingdoms there is no one like you... the Lord is the true God; he is the living God and the everlasting King." (Jeremiah 10:7, 10)

To do this, we must actively pursue this goal over time. To know anything takes time and devotion to the subject. The quality of the answer will be affected by our persistence, earnestness and sincerity. And we need a resolute desire for truth as the underlying motive.

Alfred North Whitehead, twentieth-century British scholar of logic, philosophy of science and metaphysics, said that religion must face change the same way science does. (Whitehead, 1925: 189) The principles of religion may be eternal, but the expression of those principles requires continual development ... an evolution of religious doctrine through revelation.

The important question about anything that claims to be revelation is: Does it add to our present understanding of and relationship with God? Paul states in 1Cor 14:6,12: "How will I benefit you unless I speak to you in some revelation or prophecy or teaching?... since you are eager for spiritual gifts, strive to excel in them for building up the church." And in Romans 14:19: "Let us then pursue what makes for peace and for mutual upbuilding."

Divine revelation leads to an alteration of faith—an evolution of our understanding about God. This has taken place throughout the centuries, as we see in the biblical portrayal of the patriarchs and prophets, who were each lifted to a higher spiritual realm and shown a vision:

- With Abraham, religious faith evolved to the conception of only One God.
- With Elijah, the Hebrew faith evolved to realize that God, the Creator, could never be identical with creation.
- God's revelation through Jeremiah was that each individual would have the privilege of knowing God (circumcision of the heart).
- Joel was the first to look forward to a time when everyone would be like those rare beings who are endowed with the spirit: "I will pour out my spirit on all flesh; your sons and your daughters shall prophesy, your old men shall dream dreams, and your young men shall see visions." (Joel 2:28-29)

Gerhard von Rad states this concept of progressive revelation: "The prophets ... who speak to us in these accounts were men who had been expressly called upon to abandon the fixed orders of religion which the majority of the people still considered valid." (Von Rad, 1967: 34-35)

Harry M. Buck, Professor Emeritus of Religion at Wilson College and author of many articles and books, including *People of the Lord*, adds:

The revelation of God, then, is not something sealed off from the rest of history or the world. It requires interpretation and response, and it is a continuing revelation, not ceasing at a particular point in history but going on and on, until it can be said in the Fourth Gospel, "Greater works than I [Jesus] do shall you do, because I go to the Father." (Buck, 1966: 166-167)

In our scrupulous care to avoid the pitfalls of false prophets or mediums, we must be careful not to close ourselves off to the evolution of faith through true prophetic revelation. Mediumship or spiritualism is not wrong, especially if God or a high spirit sent by God comes through. If God has revealed Himself to mortals in the past, and we can point to examples of true prophets throughout our entire human existence, then He will continue to do so.

We must develop our discernment so we can recognize the mediums who channel their own minds or lower spirits from the true prophet of God, who, because of an experience with God, has an important message to impart to humanity, strengthening and healing our faith by adding to the knowledge and understanding of God.

———— ⋇ ————

CHAPTER 5

NEW TESTAMENT AUTHORITY

"Religion is the defense against religious experience."

—Carl Jung, founder of analytical psychology, b. 1875

THE EVIDENCE IS overwhelming that pseudonymity (attributed authorship or "false name"), anonymity, and editorial additions run rampant in the New Testament. So, what determines the truth and authority of these ancient written documents? How did the early Christian Church during the formative years before and during the formation of the canon of the New Testament decide between writings considered heretical, or false, and those considered sacred, or true? Who was the authority, and what was this authority based on? What circumstances influenced the formation of a canon, or standard, of authoritative books of the New Testament? What were the criteria for selection?

Authenticity of the New Testament

American scholars Dennis C. Duling, Professor Emeritus of the Department of Religious Studies and Theology at Canisius College (specializing in social-scientific criticism of the New Testament), and Norman H. Perrin, Associate Professor of New Testament Studies at the Divinity School of the University of Chicago (specializing in redaction criticism) authored the textbook *The New Testament: Proclamation and Parenesis, Myth and History.* In this text they point out that early Christians did not accept all the traditions about Jesus. They describe various kinds of groups that emerged:

- Ultratraditionalists, who stressed Temple and Torah purity;
- Traditionalists willing to forgo circumcision but not meal purity;
- Moderate traditionalists, like Peter (who had been eating with Gentiles when his peers weren't watching);
- Reformers like Paul, who preached freedom from the Torah; and
- Radical reformers, like the Hellenists, who attacked both Temple and Torah traditionalists outright. (Duling & Perrin, 1994)

Jesus' close disciples could not even reach a consensus on how to interpret the life and teachings of Jesus. Many writings were available to choose from, representing different groups and individuals. There were also oral traditions in circulation that some considered superior to the written word.

In his book, *Introduction to the New Testament*, American scholar Helmet Koester, Professor of New Testament Studies and Ecclesiastical History at Harvard Divinity School, and a leading authority on the gospels in early Christianity, wrote that as late as 130 CE, Papias of Hierapolis "placed a higher value on the oral tradition from the apostles that was passed down by their successors than on written gospels." (Koester, 1982: 2-3)

No one can report any event except through their own presuppositions and previous experience. In the Gospel According to John, for example, the Christian faith developed out of an independent Jesus tradition that relates only slightly to the synoptic gospels of Matthew, Mark, and Luke. (Duling, 1994)

The history of oral traditions shows that as the settings and functions changed, the forms of the sayings and stories changed, and in the process, the content shifted. The parables of Jesus provide good examples. These stories, which originally challenged accepted religious and social attitudes in a particular context, were often transformed in the early church into symbolic allegories for moral teachings. (Duling, 1994)

Redaction criticism assumes that the Biblical writers were more than simple compilers of tradition. It assumes they were creative authors who intended to put forth their own perspectives or theologies. Form criticism classifies units of scripture according to literary patterns to determine the historical context. Source criticism seeks to determine the original source of the biblical text. Combining form criticism, source criticism and redaction criticism can allow one to observe how authors of Matthew and Luke, for example, made use of Q (a hypothetical lost early document of Jesus' sayings), Mark, oral traditions, and other written traditions.

Setbacks from Pseudonymity and Other Editorial Woes

We don't actually know who the writers were for most of the New Testament books. The most notable exception is Paul. In the New Testament writings, we see evidence of the existence of schools such as the Johannine School and the Pauline School, where a later author puts John's name or Paul's name on it to give it authority. Called pseudonymous writing, it was widely-practiced in antiquity. The modern notion of intellectual property had not developed yet.

Pseudonymity was fostered by writers in groups that highly regarded the person whose name was put on their documents. This phenomenon was not unique among the early Christians. Pseudonymous Jewish apocalypses written in the period before, during, and after the rise of Christianity were attributed to ancient ancestors such as Abraham and Moses. Duling & Perrin give various reasons for the occurrence of pseudonymity:

> Books were associated with an author's *opinion*, books were *believed* to have been written by an author, and books were named with the *conscious intention to give them authority*. In some cases it is difficult to be sure which reasons apply. Indeed, all three reasons could simultaneously apply: conscious attribution of an author, belief that the author wrote, and association with the author's opinions. (Duling, 1994: 261-262)

In short, pseudonymity was a common fact in early Christianity. This has important implications for the interpretation of the New Testament gospels. They were not written because Jesus' disciples heard his message, memorized it, and then wrote about it in their memoirs. Rather, unknown authors used some written source or learned it from familiar oral or liturgical traditions. (Duling, 1994)

Charles E. Carlston, Emeritus Professor of New Testament Interpretation at Andover Newton Theological School, wrote about the problems of pseudonymity in his article "The Canon—Problems and Benefits." He stated that Christian scripture gave ample evidence of the "constant revision and reappropriation of tradition," like the creation of several accounts of the life and ministry of Jesus, and, most notably, pseudonymous works. He bluntly wrote: "For many moderns—and for most modern students—it is self-evident that a pseudonymous writing is a pure and simple forgery." (Carlston, 1991: 36)

Textual Criticism

Coupled with the problems posed by pseudonymity, textual criticism shows us that throughout hundreds of years, many accidental changes have taken place in the New Testament text. The most important period during which most of the corruptions took place was during the decades immediately following the writing of the original autographs. We don't have a single fragment of an original of any New Testament book. And it is not likely that any of the most ancient surviving copies stemmed from an original autograph. (Koester, 1982)

New Testament textual scholars know that most of the corruptions occurred during the first few decades, in the period between the autograph and first edition. Koester states: "It does not make much difference how many manuscripts written since the end of II CE have been preserved, since not a single manuscript provides us with a direct insight into the history of the text during the first fifty to one hundred years after the writing of the autograph." (Koester, 1982: 41)

Getting the message right in the first place is a big problem, even if we try. Then we have intentional additions and editing, which also occurred. It is estimated that in the approximately four thousand fragments and manuscripts to the New Testament, some two hundred thousand variations exist. (Craig, 1943) According to critical analysis, when sharp breaks or dislocations occur in ancient texts with different vocabulary or ideas, they usually signal insertions by an author or later editor.

An example is Mark 4:1-35, where the introduction (4:1-2a) and conclusion (4:33-35) portray Jesus teaching a large crowd at the Sea of Galilee. Redaction critics consider these sections to be the writer's vocabulary and style. But, Mark 4:10-12, which gives the reason for speaking in parables, has a setting in which Jesus and his followers are alone, in sharp contrast with the introduction and conclusion—a clear dislocation. (Duling, 1994)

Another example of intentional additions or editing can be found in the Gospel of John. The author is not identified in the book itself except by reference in the title: "The Gospel According to John." In fact, *none* of the four gospels identifies its author within the book. The superscriptions (or titles) of the gospels, with their formula ("According to X"), were added to distinguish one from the other according to *second-century opinion*. (Duling, 1994)

If we look for information about the author of "John's" gospel within the book itself, we find some curious clues. At the end of John 21, the author says, "this is the disciple who is testifying to these things and has written them, and we know that his testimony is true." This implies that a group, a Johannine School, was writing from their recollections of the testimony of a "disciple" who had written things down, and that they were certifying that it was true.

Another possibility is that the phrase "and we know that his testimony is true" was tacked onto the original writer's sentence, "this is the disciple who is testifying to these things and has written them." In either case, we see the presence of more than one writer.

We find stronger evidence for a Johannine School of writers in Chapters 20 and 21 where there are two different endings (John 20:30-31 and John 21:24-25). Differences between the Greek of Chapters 1-20 and Chapter 21 lend further evidence. Another odd feature that implies a later writer added Chapter 21 includes the resurrection appearance of Jesus, which is located in Jerusalem in John 20, but in John 21, it takes place in Galilee.

Paul's Letters Polluted Too

Letters written by the Apostle Paul were not immune to these corruptions. A feature of some of Paul's letters are radical breaks in the flow of thought. In some cases, this can be explained by his own deviations in the course of his argument. But, in a few places, there are later insertions by either a student of Paul's or a later scribe.

For example, the attitude that women should keep silent in the churches (1Cor 14:33b-36) contradicts his views in 1Cor 11:5-12 where women are praying and prophesying along with the men. Other radical interruptions come from misplaced parts of letters— one can pick up the flow of thought a few verses, or even chapters, later. (Duling, 1994)

Six letters attributed to Paul are candidates for pseudonymity because the vocabulary, ideas, style, and social relationships differ from the seven undisputed letters of Paul. The Pastorals—1 Timothy, 2 Timothy, and Titus—are judged by almost all scholars to be pseudonymous. Ephesians is considered pseudonymous by most scholars, and Colossians and 2 Thessalonians by some. Hebrews is not by Paul, and is not part of any other known movement.

Before the fourth century, Hebrews was *not* considered to be by Paul. Origen, a theologian and scholar of Alexandria in the third century, made a famous statement about Hebrews: "But who wrote the letter, God really knows." (Duling, 1994: 282-283) Attribution to Paul came in the late fourth century. So, Hebrews was included in the canon when Augustine supported the canon of the eastern bishop Athanasius. Jerome, the famous translator of the Vulgate edition, added his agreement.

The writers of some of these pseudonymous letters were disciples of the apostle who imitated their teacher, wrote in his name, and identified themselves with him—a Pauline School. Many schools of learning existed in the Jewish and Greco-Roman world, like Plato's Academy and Epicurus' Garden. Groups like the rabbis and the Stoics were also influential. Early Christians developed schools, too, especially those who followed the ideas of Paul and the writer of the Gospel According to John. Helmut Koester wrote:

> The model of the Pauline letter was first taken up and further developed in the circles of his students. The result is the creation of the so-called deutero-Pauline letters: 2 Thessalonians, Colossians, Ephesians, the Pastoral Epistles (1 & 2 Timothy, Titus), Laodiceans, and 3 Corinthians. Not only do all of these use the model of the Pauline letters, they also continue the Pauline tradition under his authority. But soon other authors began to write under their own names, or under the names of other apostles, still using the model of the Pauline letter for their own purposes. (Koester, 1982: 3)

The Formation of the New Testament Canon

What distinguished writing as sacred versus heretical during the formation of the canon? The orthodox churches rejected a large amount of the literature that was in use by the early Christian communities. Known as the Apocrypha, these writings included many other gospels, letters attributed to Paul, acts of various apostles, and apocalypses. The archeological discovery of the Nag Hammadi Library contains, among other writings, the Gospel of Thomas (sayings attributed to Jesus), the Gospel of Peter (an account of Jesus' resurrection), and the

Secret Gospel of Mark (a longer version). (Duling, 1994) Why weren't these writings included in the official canon?

The Gnostic Dilemma

In the second century, a large contributing factor to the formation of a canon of authoritative texts was the increasing challenge of Gnostic ideas. (*Gnosis* is Greek for *knowledge.*) Gnosticism placed great emphasis on secretly revealed knowledge about God; the world; and the origin, condition, and destiny of humanity. According to Gnostic teachings, those who have this knowledge have experienced *rebirth* and become part of a privileged few who will be able to achieve salvation. For them, salvation meant liberation from our evil bodies and this evil world to return to the world of Light.

This *gnosis* can be taught through a secret ritual, but must ultimately come from above as a *call.* This highlights the importance of individual spiritual experience and *real* inner transformation, a *new birth.* The Gnostics insisted that physical baptism did not make one a Christian. Orthodox Christianity placed increasing importance on the physical act of ritualistic baptism.

Gnosticism included a body-soul dualism (mortal body-immortal soul). They believed in two different gods—the evil creator god as distinct from the good god of Light. Many Gnostics identified the Jewish creator god of Genesis with the evil god. They also saw the world as evil. This led them to reject the Jewish scriptures. And, since Gnosticism stressed that the world and body were evil, they could not accept a Savior who could assume a human body, suffer, and die. A Gnostic myth has a Redeemer who descends from the world of Light, disguises himself in a human form without becoming bodily, teaches *gnosis,* and then ascends back to the world of Light. This belief conflicted with the view that Jesus was a divine being who incarnated in the flesh, an idea that became a major part of belief for most Christians.

As this problem grew more intense, the orthodox church responded in several ways. First, it gathered an authoritative body of literature, which excluded Gnostic texts and interpretations. It also formulated an authoritative statement of faith that the Gnostics could not accept. Finally, it claimed that its leaders were real descendants of the apostles and these leaders became the source of authority in the church. The similar claim of the Gnostics, they said, was false. (Duling, 1994)

Gnostic schools liberally used the names of individual apostles as the authorities for their teachings. Koester writes:

> A number of gnostic writings or revelations claim the names of apostles … Since the formation of the concept of apostolicity, which became basic for the canon of the NT, took place in the ongoing controversy with the gnostic sects, it must be assumed that it was exactly the gnostic appeal to apostolic authority which prompted the fathers of the church to emphasize on their part the apostolicity of the orthodox writings. However… the actual theological basis of the formation of the NT canon did not quite agree with such an emphasis. (Koester, 1982: 8)

The orthodox and Gnostic battle over the soul of Christianity forced orthodoxy, with its requirements of belief in creeds and obedience to hierarchies, to define Christianity at the expense of its spiritual dimension, so it could distinguish its truth against so-called heresies. In choosing some gospels over others during canonization, important insights about Jesus' message were left out. For example, the feminine aspect has been largely missing from the New Testament. The Gnostics did not have this setback. They considered Mary

Magdalene a key figure, even claiming that Mary, not Peter, was the primary apostle.

The Challenge of Marcion

Marcion of Sinope, the son of a bishop of the Church in Asia Minor, played a major role in influencing the orthodox churches to form a canon. Marcion forced the issue of whether it was proper to continue to redact the gospel writings—to add to, edit, and rewrite according to the special concerns of a later writer. The formation of a canon put a stop to that practice.

Even though the emerging orthodox churches excommunicated and condemned Marcion as a heretic because of his radical beliefs, his missionary church during the last half of the second century was the only serious competitor to the orthodox Catholic Church. (Couliano, 1992)

In 144 CE, Marcion held a hearing before the clergy of the Christian congregations in Rome, where he flatly rejected the Old Testament for Christians. He believed Jesus had revealed the Supreme God, the God of love, and that this God of love was a different god than the creator deity of the Old Testament, because the creation was evil.

He further believed that the teachings of Jesus had been hopelessly corrupted by the Twelve but preserved by the one true apostle, Paul. Marcion saw a distinction between Paul, the thirteenth apostle, elected by Jesus Christ and by God, and the twelve apostles elected by the *man* Jesus. Marcion maintained that this made Paul superior to the Twelve. (Couliano, 1992)

Marcion saw the opposition between the one true apostle, Paul, and the "false apostles" as the conflict of authority that existed between Paul and the emerging Christian church in Jerusalem. He held the

Twelve in very low esteem because he thought they ignored the truth. Paul was the only apostle of Jesus Christ, and his message the only true gospel. Marcion held that false Christians had concocted the other gospels and had altered a written gospel of Paul's until it became unrecognizable as the "Gospel of Luke." (Couliano, 1992)

To support his teaching, Marcion depended on the ten-letter collection of the Pauline corpus and an edited version of the Gospel of Luke that he believed was Paul's gospel, written by Paul's companion. He edited his text of Luke and the Pauline letters, attempting to smooth away all contradictions according to the principle that the god preached by the New Testament was different from the god of the Old Testament. (Couliano, 1992) In the process, something new occurred—a set of authoritative writings distinct from the Jewish scriptures. Koester shines more light:

> Marcion, however, came to the conviction that these writings were not preserved in their original form. He therefore made a critical edition to purify the books of his canon from all later additions. Before censuring Marcion because of his critical purification of the Pauline letters, one should remember that Marcion's opponents also tried to correct the image of Paul transmitted in the genuine letters, not least by the addition of the Pastoral Epistles... Marcion's new edition of Luke conforms with a wide-spread custom of his time: Luke itself (as also Matthew) was already a new edition of the older Gospel of Mark. Thus Marcion's treatment of the Christian writings which he used for his canon was quite in agreement with the general attitude of his time. (Koester, 1982: 8-9)

Marcion's uniqueness was in elevating his edited Christian writings to the status of Holy Scripture, while at the same time rejecting the Old Testament. He was convinced that he was continuing a development started by Paul, the only true apostle. The result was Marcion's canon—the first Christian canon of scripture. This was new because it replaced the Old Testament, the recognized canon of the church. (Koester, 1982)

Marcion maintained that Christ's body was a deceiving apparition. Therefore, Christ did not die and did not rise from the dead. He also held that Jesus Christ was *not* the Messiah that the Jews were looking for and denied that the Old Testament could have been a systematic forecast of the coming of Christ. No wonder he was excommunicated! His views did not mesh with the orthodox Church's emphasis on Jesus in the flesh, the resurrected Christ, and the fulfillment of Old Testament prophecy.

The Impact of Montanus

In the middle of the second century, shortly after Marcion forced the issue of a canon, a former priest named Montanus forced the issue of a *closed* canon, where no more books could be added.

Montanus had a spiritual experience that formed the basis for an apocalyptic movement called Montanism. His spiritual experiences included falling into a trance and speaking in tongues. He claimed to be the mouthpiece of God (Heine, 1992), and a successor to Abraham and Moses, among other prophets of the Old Testament (Actemeier, 1983). He announced that he was the inspired instrument of a new outpouring of the Holy Spirit, the 'Paraclete' promised in the Gospel of John. (John 14:15-17 & 17:7-15; Metzger, 1989)

American scholar Paul J. Achtemeier, Professor Emeritus of Biblical Interpretation at Union Theological Seminary, an authority on the New Testament, authored eighteen books and over sixty journal articles. In his epilogue, "The New Testament Becomes Normative," in Howard Kee's *Understanding the New Testament*, he states that Montanus "represented a significant alternative to the other Christian communities, which were becoming increasingly institutionalized" because he "claimed powers promised in a writing that was widely accepted as authoritative (the Gospel of John) and seemed to renew the early fervor of the Christian movement." (Actemeier, 1983)

Montanism arose when the Church was consolidating its authority in bishops, creed, and canon. The movement spread fast and was soon in Rome as well as in North Africa. It produced a large body of literature and won many converts, among them the Church Father, Tertullian. (Achtemeier, 1983) At first perplexed, the majority of Church leaders in Asia Minor declared the new prophecy to be the work of demons, and excommunicated the Montanists. (Metzger, 1989)

The question of *new revelation* was at the center of the debate in North Africa and Rome. Ronald E. Heine, Professor of Bible and Christian Ministry at Northwest Christian University, authored several books on classical Christian doctrine. In his article "Montanus, Montanism" he wrote that Tertullian and the Catholic Church both acknowledged continuation of the operation of divine grace in the Church. Tertullian, however, accused the Catholics of fixing "boundaries for God." He affirmed that Christian discipline is evolving through the continued activity of revelation "to direct discipline, to reveal the Scriptures, to reform the understanding, [and] to advance the understanding to better things." (Heine, 1992: 901)

A battle ensued over the right of the Montanists to spread their teachings by appealing to the authority of the Spirit. In the end, it was this issue of authority which caused Montanism to be declared a heresy. Achtemeier stated:

The Christians could not deny that the Holy Spirit had been promised to them, but they could, and did, deny Montanus's claim that the Spirit spoke as authoritatively through him as it had through the apostles of Christ. But to do that, the Christian community had to affirm that the apostolic period set the standards for the understanding of any further communications from the Spirit. Since the followers of Montanus also produced a body of literature, the Christian communities that opposed him had to affirm that only those writings which drew directly on apostolic traditions were authoritative, and were therefore the norm for the faith of the community. (Achtemeier, 1983: 372-373)

In Phrygia, the debate about the Montanist prophecy centered on how it was done. The possibility of prophecy itself did not enter the debate. Heine wrote:

The opponents in Phrygia attempted to prove that Montanus was a false prophet because he prophesied in a state of ecstasy. Epiphanius sets this as the major topic. 'Let us examine,' he says, 'what constitutes prophecy and what constitutes false prophecy.' He argues that true prophets in both the OT and NT were always in possession of their understanding when they uttered their prophecies. (Heine, 1992: 899)

Since Montanus had an apocalyptic outlook and had used the books of John and Revelation to support his claims, some Christian communities no longer gave these writings the authoritative status they had enjoyed for over a century. (Achtemeier, 1983)

None of the many writings of Montanus and the movement called Montanism have survived. Bruce M. Metzger, famous American

New Testament scholar, translator of the 1990 *New Revised Standard Version of the Bible* and author of dozens of books on Biblical study, speculated that the writings were probably eliminated because of later imperial decrees that ordered the destruction of all Montanist codices. (Metzger, 1989)

The Clout of Constantine

Powerful and wealthy people with individual or political ambitions had great influence over the execution, dissemination, preservation, and content of written documents in early Christian times. Writing was very expensive and laborious and could only be undertaken by those with time and financial resources.

About 332 CE, the Roman Emperor Constantine directed Eusebius, bishop of Caesarea and former church historian, to have fifty copies of the "sacred Scriptures" produced. He promised to pay all expenses. Constantine was aware of the great political power to be gained by uniting the various Christian factions. He pushed for a compilation of their writings into one book in a way never before agreed to by the various churches or by Eusebius himself.

Roy Hoover, Professor of Religion Emeritus at Whitman College, and author of *How the Books of the New Testament were Chosen,* stated that the canon "was settled for all practical purposes when Constantine gave the order to create 50 Bibles. Palpable evidence of the unity of the church, their publication also symbolized the unity of the empire." (Hoover, 1993: 47)

Hoover revealed that Eusebius used historical, literary, and doctrinal criteria when he drew up his list of canonical books. The criteria were:

- Whether earlier generations of Church leaders mentioned the writings (a historical criterion),

- Whether a book's style comports well with those known to have been written early in the history of the church (a literary criterion), and
- Whether their content is consistent with established orthodoxy (a doctrinal or theological criterion). (Hoover, 1993)

Hoover further asserted that the fourth century canon "has been durable, but it has never been universal." (Hoover, 1993: 47) He cited the Syrian Church's differing canon. And Martin Luther who, in the sixteenth century, "thought James, Jude and Revelation unfit to be included among the canonical books."

The Roman Catholic Church did not issue an authoritative statement about the contents of the Bible until 1546 at the Council of Trent. With a vote of twenty-four to fifteen, with sixteen abstentions, the writings in Jerome's fourth-century Latin Vulgate version were declared the Church's official canon. Hoover writes: "In short, no single canon has ever been accepted by all Christians. In fact, the status of the New Testament canon today resembles what it was in Eusebius' day: a question that attracts both a considerable consensus and continuing differences." (Hoover, 1993: 47)

Should the New Testament Canon Be Revised?

When Martin Luther King, Jr. was assassinated in 1968, a group of ministers brought up the issue of altering the New Testament canon. They wanted to include King's 'Letter from a Birmingham Jail', written when he was in solitary confinement for participating in a civil-rights protest. He responded to white clergymen who criticized King and his followers for provoking civil disturbances. This included his good friend evangelist Billy Graham.

Instead of retreating, as he had done in the past, King wrote a letter from jail, as the apostle Paul had done, defending his actions and rebuking his critics. He began: "Seldom, if ever, do I pause to answer criticism of my work and ideas." King went on to write an eloquent and convincing essay that justified the strategy of the civil rights struggle. He confronted the conscience of mainstream America. In the process, he wrote a convincing epistle for a distinct time and place that had universal meaning for all places and times.

According to Bruce Metzger, King's letter was considered because it "conveys a strong prophetic witness, and interprets God's will in the spirit of Christ." (Metzger, 1989: 271) The decision was not to add the letter to the canon because of the vast differences in age and character between it and the New Testament books. Metzger further pointed out:

> Suggestions that the canon might be enlarged by the inclusion of other 'inspirational' literature, ancient or modern, arise from a failure to recognize what the New Testament actually is. It is not an anthology of inspirational literature; it is a collection of writings that bear witness to what God has wrought through the life and work, the death and resurrection of Jesus Christ, and through the founding of his Church by his Spirit. (Metzger, 1989: 271)

Something from the past like the Dead Sea Scrolls could still be unearthed. But Metzger says if it doesn't add to what's already in the New Testament, it should not be added to the canon. An example of a text that could be included is the Gospel of Thomas because it enhances our understanding of the gospel traditions circulating after Jesus' death. A collection of 114 sayings attributed to Jesus and allegedly written by the Apostle Thomas, it is not actually a gospel. But it is important because it contains a very old gospel tradition not directly taken from our canonical gospels but derived from another source.

Charles E. Carlston, Professor Emeritus of New Testament Interpretation at Andover Newton Theological School, in his article "The canon—problems and benefits," affirms that the question of the Christian canon is still open because the original justification for a canon has broken down. "Yet both scholars and ordinary church members go on using it," he wrote, "as if the theoretical problem were irrelevant—or even unknown!" (Carlston, 1991: 33) He explained:

> In the early church… the formation of the NT canon was a gradual process of both inclusion and exclusion, and it rested on a number of principles, which we might describe schematically as reducible to three: apostolic provenance, widespread use, and theological orthodoxy. In our very historically minded age, all three principles have been seriously (and rightly) challenged in a way that the earliest church could hardly have imagined. (Carlston, 1991: 33)

First, Carlston addresses the principle of apostolic provenance: "Who today would argue seriously that all twenty-seven books of the NT come, directly or indirectly, from those close followers of Jesus that we call 'apostles'?" He cites convincing evidence that of the twenty-seven New Testament books, not more than seven or eight are apostolic (*at most* fourteen). It still looks to most contemporary interpreters, he says, "as if Matthew rests on the Gospel of Mark, itself increasingly interpreted without any reference to Peter, its supposed 'apostolic' source." (Carlston, 1991: 33-34)

The other two criteria don't get much support from Carlston either. On the criteria of use, he says even though the underlying impulse is valid, this criterion is very hard to evaluate with any precision. He further reveals that the churches of Eastern and Western Europe "have never agreed on just which books meet this particular canon. And... it hardly seems appropriate to ignore the even more extensive canon of Ethiopic churches. So clearly 'widespread use' is elusive, however central it may be." (Carlston, 1991: 34)

Similarly, he considers the criterion of orthodoxy to be "elusive, probably even misleading." Orthodoxy does not recognize the original roots of movements considered heretical. So, they misunderstand their actual origin and development. At the same time the orthodox church idealizes the unity of the early church. Carlston asserts: "Further—and worse—the 'priority of orthodoxy' criterion does not deal adequately with the fact that our present canon reflects political and social factors at work in the battle over Gnosticism and other movements in the second and third centuries." (Carlston, 1991: 34)

Carlston points out that the original decisions about the canon were based on "scholarly judgments, episcopal decisions, liturgical acts in hundreds of congregations scattered in time and space, and so on." (Carlston, 1991: 35) He also emphasizes that it was the groups who held power who defined what was heretical and marginal.

On the problem of re-defining and re-shaping the canon, Carlston states: "In the long run, a church that cannot be defined, or one that defines itself only from within, will be unable to lay claim to being a faithful transmitter of that tradition in which it purports to stand." (Carlston, 1991: 40)

Implications for Modern Times

Today many sincere Christians accept the New Testament books as authoritative. But they have fallen victim to many of the same forces that branded Jesus and his teachings blasphemous and heretical in his own time: religious and political leaders, corruptions, dogmas, and rituals. If Jesus were to present himself in our day, would we recognize him or his teachings?

New Testament scholar, Father Raymond E. Brown, whose Jewish and Christian research in several ancient and modern languages, along with assessing the work of more than two thousand scholars for his two-volume study, *The Death of the Messiah*, wrote: "Jesus was widely seen as a disturber of the religious structures of his time. Were Jesus to appear in our own day, he would probably be arrested and tried again. Most of those finding him guilty would identify themselves as Christians, and think they were rejecting an imposter." (Woodward, 1994: 53)

Concerning the grounds on which Jesus was arrested, Brown states: "Jesus did something to threaten the temple, which was at the center of Jerusalem's economic life. And any threat to the temple was of grave political concern to Rome." (Woodward, 1994: 51)

In Paul's life and ministry, we see a pious Jew, a Pharisee, protecting and defending his own sacred tradition by trying to stop a radical band of blasphemers, now known as Christians. In the midst of this zealous persecution, Paul succumbs to a spiritual experience that reveals information and authority from the spirit of Jesus himself. "For I want you to know, brothers and sisters, that the gospel that was proclaimed by me is not of human origin; for I did not receive it from a human source, nor was I taught it, but I received it through a revelation of Jesus Christ." (Gal 1:11) And in 1Cor 15:8, after noting resurrection appearances to Cephas, the Twelve, five hundred brethren, James, and "all the apostles," Paul states, "Last of all, as to one untimely born, he appeared also to me."

The power of this spiritual experience transformed him to become a foremost leader and authority among the Christians he had been persecuting, without any formal training in Jesus' teachings or certificate of ordination. Paul had never known Jesus as a man, which was a necessary component of being an apostle for the author of Luke–Acts (Acts 1:21-26). Paul encountered delicate problems in his claim to be an apostle to the Gentiles because of this fact. His authority was often challenged, especially in Galatia and Corinth. Paul argued that his apostleship was not of human origin: "Paul an apostle—sent neither by human commission nor from human authorities, but through Jesus Christ and God the Father" (Gal 1:1).

Outside agitators of Jewish background (2 Cor 11:22) with "letters of recommendation" (2 Cor 3:1-3) came to Corinth. Paul scorned them as "superlative apostles" (2 Cor 3:1, 11:4-5, 11) and said they were really "false apostles." Paul accused them of being "deceitful workers, disguising themselves as apostles of Christ" (2 Cor 11:13). They, too, claimed to be apostles, and thus competitors for leadership at Corinth. Paul said they preached "another Jesus" and had "a different spirit" (2 Cor 11:4). These "super apostles" were also performing miracles, and Paul's response was that he, too, was a miracle worker. (Duling, 1994) "For such boasters are false apostles, deceitful workers, disguising themselves as apostles of Christ. And no wonder! Even Satan disguises himself as an angel of light. So it is not strange if his ministers also disguise themselves as ministers of righteousness." (2 Cor 11:13-15)

These "super apostles" were likely apostles such as Peter or James who carried great authority in the Jerusalem church. Paul was possibly accusing original disciples of Jesus of being workers of Satan!

The gift of the Spirit in the Christian community in Galatia was one of the proofs that Paul used to assert his authority. Prophecy was a high gift, and there is evidence that early Christians believed the "spirit of Jesus" or the "spirit of Christ" was speaking through their prophets. Helmut Koester wrote that from the beginning there was an oral tradition transmitted "under the authority of the 'Lord'," comprised of sayings of Jesus and short stories. Not only sayings of the man Jesus, but the words of the "risen Lord." (Koester, 1982)

Duling and Perrin also pointed out the prominence of prophecy in early Christianity, especially the Q community. This group, one of the earliest communities of Jesus' followers, circulated a gospel composed of sayings of Jesus, referred to as "Q" by biblical scholars. Scholars believe this gospel, which no longer exists, was one of the main sources used by the original writers of the gospels attributed to Matthew, Mark, Luke, and John. Duling and Perrin wrote that the Q community was led by "spirit-filled, eschatological prophets who spoke for the now departed, but soon to return, Jesus. Prophecy, then, was one of the chief characteristics of the emergent community." (Duling, 1994: 152)

If early Christians accepted these prophetic expressions as being inspired by the spirit of Jesus or John, why can't Christians accept that the spirit of Jesus or John could still be operating through prophets today? Isn't the spirit of Jesus still alive and functioning today as it was in Paul's time? Couldn't someone like Paul appear in our own day?

Today there are millions of Pauls. According to Roy L. Hill, PsyD, in *Jesus and the Near-Death Experience*, 15 million people in the United States alone have had an NDE or OBE. (Hill, 2017) And the person seen most often during these experiences is Jesus.

———— ✦ ————

CHAPTER 6

NDES AND OBES

"There is nothing so powerful as truth, and often nothing so strange."

—Daniel Webster, American orator and politician, b. 1782

IS THERE LIFE after death? Most religions include a belief in the afterlife, and speculation about this question escapes no one. But some of us are able to go beyond the point of speculation.

It is now an established medical fact that a person can suffer cardiac arrest, stop breathing and lose all brain activity, yet still fully recover. Dr. Eben A. Alexander is a radical example.

"[He] is living proof of an afterlife," states Dr. Raymond A. Moody, Jr., the physician, psychologist, philosopher, and author who is the widely-regarded pioneer of NDE research. He further states that Dr. Alexander's "near-death experience is the most astounding I have heard in more than four decades of studying this phenomenon." (Alexander, 2012: cover) It was Dr. Moody who first coined the term near-death experience in his best-selling 1975 book *Life After Life*, a classic in its contribution to our understanding of what happens when and after we die and the implications of those discoveries.

Dr. Alexander was a neurosurgeon, a materialist scientist, who was of the popular opinion that, even though NDEs might feel real, they were simply fantasies produced by a brain under extreme stress. Then, in November of 2008, he had his own NDE. He contracted a rare, deadly form of meningitis and went into a coma while the bacterial infection ravaged the physical brain matter that controls thought and emotion. He had no brain activity whatsoever and was expected to die.

Seven days after lapsing into the coma, as his doctors were about to stop treatment, he awoke and recovered.

While in the coma, Dr. Alexander had a profound spiritual experience with the world beyond the physical that convinced him that his previously-held conviction about NDEs as a highly-trained neurosurgeon, was all wrong. His book, *Proof of Heaven*, is one of the best I have read, on any subject, among the hundreds I have read in the past several years. His case proves the independence of consciousness from the body.

As of June 2019, one out of ten people have had an NDE according to the European Academy of Science, as reported on the History Channel (August 31, 2019) in *The UnXplained: Mysterious Phenomena*. *Millions* of people, some as young as three years old, have recovered from death to tell us what happened.

These survivors are scouts of a world beyond death, peering into the afterlife, speaking out in numbers science cannot ignore. And they come back with the certainty that there is life after death. Their reports are a wake-up call that our individual consciousness continues after death, and we experience a change in form from physical to spiritual.

A classic NDE begins with an out-of-body experience (OBE) where you find yourself peering into another reality or through another reality from a non-attached perspective outside the body. Often there is a tunnel with a light at the far end that becomes increasingly more beautiful and brilliant. The colors are more vivid and luminous than on earth. You feel like you could stay in the light, in the calm, in the happiness and radiant joy, forever.

Time is transformed. In one instant you can review your entire life. In another instant you can become imbued with enough vision to go beyond what you could ever hope to accomplish in a lifetime. Loved ones who have passed over appear to greet you. And often you feel a profoundly loving, accepting, benign presence ... a presence who knows you completely.

Rev. Angus H. Haddow, Chairman of the Churches' Fellowship for Psychical and Spiritual Studies in Scotland, writes about the "Being of Light"—"a personal being who emanates love and warmth." It has a profound effect on those who see it. Christians often identify this entity with Jesus. Haddow says a "direct transfer of thought takes place between the person who has the NDE and the Being of Light." (Haddow, 1991: 80)

He also mentions the similarity between the encounter with the Being of Light and Paul's conversion experience on the road to Damascus. "Although Paul's experience probably was not an NDE, the bright light was seen, he heard the voice, and Paul's life was changed by that encounter. And parallels with the encounter with the bright light are even clearer in the Egyptian Book of the Dead and the Tibetan Book of the Dead." (Haddow, 1991: 80-81)

In an article entitled "Out-of-Body and Near-Death Experiences: Their Impact on Religious Beliefs," Haddow summarizes the available data on these experiences. He stresses the potential usefulness of these events in many areas: spirituality studies, philosophy, psychology, theology, and personal spirituality. Those who have a near-death experience "are so affected by it that they remember every detail, and their attitudes to God and to death can change as a result." (Haddow, 1991: 75)

Haddow describes the OBE as a sensation of being a spectator who looks down on his body, with "a lack of sensation of body weight, movement, and position sense." Instantaneous movement happens from place to place. Physical objects present no barrier to movement. Hearing and seeing become more acute.

OBEs do not occur only during NDEs, but they can happen spontaneously during other activities like sleep, unconsciousness following anesthesia, and stress. If you have a spontaneous OBE, you are likely to draw the conclusion that you possess a soul, linked to a spirit body, separate from the physical body, that will survive physical death with full consciousness. "Death would then be an OBE in which one did not succeed in getting back into his body," states Haddow. "This conclusion is often drawn by those who experience NDEs.... He has, it seems to him, learned by experience what it is like to die." (Haddow, 1991: 76)

Dutch scientists weighed the physical body before, during and after OBEs and found a loss of 2–1/4 ounces during an OBE. (Zammit, 2013: 35)

NDE Pioneers

Dr. Raymond Moody was the first to explore near-death experiences in the 1970s. (Moody, 1975) He isolated fifteen separate elements that occurred in these experiences. Eight to twelve of these elements occurred in the majority of NDEs:

- Ineffability–no words can express the sacredness of the experience

- Hearing the "death" pronouncement
- Feelings of peace and quiet
- Unusual auditory sensations
- A dark tunnel
- Experiencing being out of the body (OBE)
- Meeting others
- A being of indescribable brilliance and love
- A panoramic life review
- A border or limit
- Coming back
- Conviction of the reality of the experience
- New goals and moral principles
- New views of death
- Corroboration of witnesses and/or events

Many other researchers have confirmed his findings, including Elisabeth Kübler-Ross, a University of Chicago professor and psychiatrist who studied the emotional impact of confronting death, and lectured to the medical profession on the subject. In 1976, independently of Moody's research, she came to conclusions that paralleled Moody's findings and deduced that death is just a transition, "a peaceful and benign experience common to all cultures in which the physical body is shed… as a butterfly comes out of a cocoon. (Haddow 1991: 76)

Kenneth Ring, professor of psychology at the University of Connecticut at Storrs, provides pioneering and detailed research on NDEs in his book *Life at Death* and his article "Further Studies of the Near-Death Experience." He found that many cases of NDEs involved OBEs, and that almost everyone who had an NDE declared the experience to be pleasant. "The individuals who had NDEs became convinced that the values of love and service to others were more important than material comforts; that religion had become more meaningful to them, and that death was not to be feared." (Haddow, 1991: 76)

OBEs in the Bible

Out-of-body experiences are also mentioned in the Bible. The Apostle Paul refers to the "spiritual body," which has a parallel with the "second body," in its immateriality and its lack of physical limitations (1 Cor 15:35-52). This second or spiritual body is often called *soul body, etheric body, astral body,* or *etheric double.* Paul even refers to being "out of the body" twice in 2 Cor 12:2-4:

> I know a person in Christ who fourteen years ago was caught up to the third heaven—whether in the body or out of the body I do not know; God knows. And I know that such a person—whether in the body or out of the body I do not know; God knows—was caught up into Paradise and heard things that are not to be told, that no mortal is permitted to repeat.

The concept that human beings have more than one body was also held by the ancient Egyptians and is currently part of the Tibetan Buddhist faith. (Haddow, 1991) The *spiritual body* is also in the Biblical account of the transfiguration of Jesus on the mountain when he went to pray with his disciples Peter, James, and John (Matthew 17:2-7):

> And he was transfigured before them, and his face shone like the sun, and his clothes became dazzling white. Suddenly there appeared to them Moses and Elijah, talking with him... While

he was still speaking, suddenly a bright cloud overshadowed them, and from the cloud a voice said, "This is my Son, the Beloved; with him I am well pleased; listen to him!" When the disciples heard this, they fell to the ground and were overcome by fear. But Jesus came and touched them, saying, "Get up and do not be afraid." And when they looked up, they saw no one except Jesus himself alone.

These features of light, of seeing deceased spirits, and of hearing spoken words, also occur in NDEs. Could these experiences be a doorway to death, or just a movie our brains run during times of extreme stress?

What's Happening?

No one doubts that these survivors believe what they say, but some scientists say psychological and physiological processes are the cause, that it is a chemical event in a dying brain producing large amounts of endorphins.

But there are things that cannot be explained by these theories. Scientists like Eben Alexander, who themselves have had NDEs, find that science cannot touch many areas of the experience, such as feelings of love, awe, and faith in God. These scientists say there is no explanation other than it being a real, valid experience.

Haddow states that even though consciousness feels normal except for the sensation of being out-of-the-body, "NDEs and OBEs may be dismissed as some sort of hallucination or altered state of consciousness.... But this reasoning seldom affects persons who have had NDEs and who thus become convinced that they will survive physical death." (Haddow 1991: 82) A hallucination will register on an EEG, but Eben Alexander's EEGs were flat—no brain activity whatsoever. Yet Dr. Alexander's consciousness was still very much active. And people who have hallucinated don't describe it as spiritual transformation.

The famous psychologist Carl G. Jung, protégé of Sigmund Freud, almost died in an OBE. He writes about the reality of his experience:

> I would never have imagined that any such experience was possible. It was not a product of imagination. The visions or experiences were utterly real; there was nothing subjective about them; they all had a quality of absolute objectivity...
> I can describe the experience only as the ecstasy of a non-temporal state in which past, present, and future are one...
> The experience might have been defined as a state of feeling, but one which cannot be produced by imagination. (Haddow, 1991: 82)

Emanuel Swedenborg, 18th-century European scientist, philosopher, theologian, Lutheran mystic, and nobleman, had a prolific career as an inventor and mining engineer. At the age of fifty-three he turned from science to theology. He published eighteen theological works, including *True Christian Religion* and *Heaven and Hell*. He was adamant about the validity of his OBE experiences, where he was given a conducted tour of Heaven and Hell:

> I am well aware that many will say that no one can possibly speak with angels so long as he lives in the body, and many will say that it is all a phantasy, others that I related such things in order to gain credence, and others will make other objections. But by all this I am not deterred, for I have seen, I have heard, I have felt. (Haddow, 1991:82-3)

———— ➤⊰⊱ ————

My OBEs

I had my first out-of-body experience in 1968, during my first year of college at Washington State University. I was living in a dormitory, and one night in the bathroom, I got dizzy and felt faint. I had just experienced the trauma of an unsuccessful attempt to use a tampon. For the first time. It was awful.

I gathered my belongings by the sink and made for the door. Conveniently, my bedroom door was right across the hall, but between the bathroom door and my bedroom door, my consciousness left my body.

As I slowly collapsed to the floor, I rose up out of my body and watched it fall to the ground…as I floated gently…to the bathroom ceiling. Going back in time, I watched myself in the bathroom from moments prior, observing, until I started to fall in the hallway. I floated back into my body, picked up my toiletries, arose from the floor, went into my bedroom, set everything down, and went immediately to bed. Exhausted, I soon drifted off to sleep.

In the middle of the night, I awakened to the sensation of my body feeling heavy, like a lead weight. But when I opened my eyes, I found myself, my consciousness, in a spirit body. Hovering over my physical body. Parallel to it. Like levitation.

The next moment I was back in my body, after noticing this brief separation.

These experiences demonstrated to me that I, my consciousness, my spirit, was not my body. Yet, they were not sufficient to overcome a growing agnosticism. I wanted proof that God existed, and I challenged Him to prove it to me. I spent many years pleading with God for proof, but did not get an answer that swayed me from agnosticism, until October 26, 1974.

———— ➤✦◄ ————

Encounter with God: Testimony of Author

I swear to God that what I am about to share with you is all true.

I will never forget the day I met my Maker. My life changed forever. And my death. And for a second, the beginning was almost the end.

I had never heard of a near-death experience when I had one on October 26, 1974. It changed my whole life. It changed how I look at life, and what I want to do with my life. I have no fear of death now, but instead look forward to the peace, love, and joy it will bring—and freedom from material bondage. That does not mean I have a death wish. Instead, I am more alive than ever, with a purpose beyond myself.

I was an agnostic before that day. For several years I had been challenging God to prove to me that He existed, but I had received no answer... until *that* day. On *that* day, God intervened to save my life. On *that* day I was instantly transformed from an agnostic into a person of unwavering faith, willing to do *anything* for God.

On that auspicious October day, I lived in Shaker Heights, Ohio in a three-family home. My husband and I lived on the second floor, and we had tenants on the first and third floors. On the third floor, lived a brother and sister, Mike and Emelie (names changed), who had resided there for twenty-seven years. They were in their eighties, and Mike held the world record at that time for the number of pacemakers put in one's body. About once a year Mike would have an attack, necessitating a new pacemaker.

One day while I was talking with Emelie, we heard a loud thud upstairs and hurried up to investigate. We found Mike collapsed on the floor. He appeared to be dead. I called 911 for help, then tried to help Emelie resuscitate him, but to no avail. Mike had not had a heart attack, but had died of a stroke.

In the following weeks, Emelie became very dependent on me for support and companionship, at a time when we were making the decision to move to a different city for my husband's job as a college textbook salesman.

Several months later, we moved to Akron, Ohio, which meant selling the home in Shaker Heights. We took our time finding the right buyer, a very sensitive couple, informed of Emelie's situation and dependencies, and willing to support her.

I set up a meeting for Emelie to meet the new owners, and when they arrived, I called her, which had been our pre-arrangement. But as soon as I identified myself, she hung up on me. I went to her door and knocked.

When the door opened, there stood Emelie with a butcher knife raised above her head, and her eyes were dark, zombie-like, glazed-over. She looked crazy enough in that moment to plunge the knife right into my chest.

Suddenly, a tremendous power came into the environment. I could feel it in me and it felt like it was all around me ... a power so wonderful and awesome that it felt greater than anything I had ever felt. It was a loving presence so enormous it felt like all the love I had ever felt in my entire lifetime amplified by a billion ... yet the blissful Love that I felt from that power was greater than that!

I could see that it affected Emelie as well, for the arm that held the knife began to melt to her side, and an expression of great calm and peace came over her. The situation was immediately transformed from the threat of imminent violence to one of harmony, gentleness, oneness, and, predominantly, Love.

I didn't even have time to be afraid. It all happened in an instant. This Love transformed my essence. And I *knew* that this Love was God. I was no longer an agnostic. My faith was unshakeable from *that* day on.

I told the buyers of our home what had happened. They were amazed by the experience, and were not deterred from purchasing the home.

Ecstatic experiences and revelations continued, and I felt called to communicate these experiences through visual art. My husband, a college textbook salesman, supported me in becoming an artist, yet could never fully support my interest in the spirit world. He couldn't understand the enthusiastic expressions of intense joy these experiences awoke in my soul. He took me to a psychiatrist for evaluation, but due to the nature of psychiatry at that time, there was no diagnostic code for "spiritual or religious problems."

This deficiency did not change until May 1994 when the fourth edition of the American Psychiatric Association's "Diagnostic and Statistical Manual" (DSM) came out. The DSM included a diagnostic code called "spiritual or religious problem." For the first time in the profession of psychiatry, there was clarification that spiritual or religious problems are not necessarily symptomatic of a mental disorder. Psychiatrist Stanislav Grof, author of *Spiritual Emergency: When Transformation Becomes a Crisis* and *The Stormy Search for the Self: A Guide to Personal Growth through Transformational Crisis*, stated: "We became aware that some of the experiences we've labeled as psychotic have been stages of transformation instead." (Oldenburg, 1994: col. 2)

Psychologist Emma Bragdon, author of *A Source Book for Helping People with Spiritual Problems*, stated that few therapists have any education or experience in dealing with spiritual emergencies. Bragdon pointed out that "the extreme looks very much like psychotic break-down," often with manic behavior. Many people "have been misdiagnosed and treated inappropriately—which means they've been medicated or hospitalized, which obstructs what the spiritual emergence is all about." (Oldenburg, 1994: col. 3)

This sounds almost identical to my own experience. The psychiatrist diagnosed me as having a psychotic breakdown with a manic condition. He recommended hospitalization for a few days of rest, but when we got to the hospital, fortunately, there were no beds available. I was forced to receive an injection of the drug Haldol, which, before we arrived home, was already beginning to cause agonizing muscle spasms in my entire upper body. I had been given a drug for a condition I did not have, and got no relief from the pain until I went back to the hospital for a dose of a counteracting drug.

Although traumatized by this response to my spiritual emergence, my constant prayers and daily testing of the validity of my experiences left me with the realization that I felt more exuberant about life, love, and being an educated, creative person than ever before.

Above all this, I also felt a growing relationship with God and Jesus and a steadfast faith in that Higher Love, which was so magical. I quickly stopped going to the psychiatrist. I didn't think we needed to be paying $75 per hour for me to teach him what was *really* happening to me. I *knew* my connection with God was good and healthy for me. It gave my life a purpose, meaning, and happiness I had never known.

Following the calling to be an artist, I pursued studio art at Kent State University, five years after the deadly shootings of student protesters by our country's armed forces. I continued to have spiritually transformative experiences (STEs), and channeled them into artworks. Always accompanied by God's Love, these STEs included a clairsentient, clairaudient and claircognizant meeting with Jesus. And premonitions about a new version of the Bible, or separate New Testament, inspired or written by Jesus. This, my first call to discipleship, was in November 1976.

In March of 1980, my cousin, David Olson, a chiropractic doctor in Encinitas, California, invited me for a visit. During my stay, I felt a welcoming acceptance and understanding of spiritual emergence within my cousin's circle of friends and Yogananda's Self-Realization Fellowship. Feeling more and more drawn to this supportive atmosphere, I decided to move there. I told my husband of my decision and, of course, wanted him to come. He declined. We cordially parted ways, over spiritual and religious differences.

Three thousand miles away, in Washington D.C., a young man named Jonathan Sperry felt guided to move to Encinitas, California, in the same month and year. We kept mysteriously crossing paths, then discovered that we lived on the same street, a few blocks apart.

One day we decided to sit down and get to know one another. As we shared our spiritual journeys and experiences, it became clear we needed to talk further. At our next meeting, Jonathan said he was guided to share a book with me that had been crucial to his spiritual path. He gave me one of four volumes of automatic writings received by James E. Padgett entitled *True Gospel Revealed Anew by Jesus*.

I instantly recognized the writings as genuine. Jesus had already told me about them. I brought them to my heart, prayed to God in gratitude, and received an inflowing of His Love. Then I felt the spirit of Jesus with us. I had not felt his presence since November 1976. "This is what I was telling you about," he whispered to my soul. This was my second calling.

———→❊←———

Dance with Jesus

Remember the Beatles? Remember Beatlemaniacs? Well, I was one. Yes, a screaming Beatlemaniac. I was such a big fan that I had to have a new album on the day it came out. Paul McCartney was my favorite, and when the Beatles broke up, I continued to follow Paul and his band *Wings*. The day their album '*Wings at the Speed of Sound*' came out, I immediately purchased it, brought it home, and put it on my diamond-needle record player.

My husband was out of town for business, so I was by myself. I would be free to enjoy the new album and dance to my heart's content, without any witnesses to my dorky self-expression. The music was so inspiring, and I was having so much fun! Music is a super-power—and so is dance. I was in a state of ecstasy, and, suddenly, as the song '*Let 'Em In*' started, the spirit of Jesus was dancing with me!

I danced with Jesus until I became exhausted, then I plopped down on the couch, grabbed my sketch pad, and started to make notations about visions and information I was receiving. At one point, a breeze came through the room, strong enough to whisk papers from my desk. But there were no windows open, and no fan going. It was November in Akron, Ohio. A wind came from nowhere—like ten years earlier when Abraham Lincoln appeared behind me on the wall.

Jesus enlightened me about mistakes in the Bible, and how things had been added in that were not true. Corrections needed to be made. I thought I was being given the task of making these corrections, but this felt beyond me. And it was.

That's not what Jesus had in mind. He was impressing me about Bible errors, and that more information was available, directly from him. Six years later, when I was introduced to Padgett's mediumship and presented with the messages from Jesus, Jesus came to me again to verify them and let me know that this is what he had been talking about!

How did I know it was Jesus?

His presence told me. There was no question. I could feel his authority and regal power, as well as his great love, humility, and grace. I just knew. Both times. And there have been other times when Jesus visited me and I have known it was him. This is an aspect of precognition—you just know, without knowing why or how you know.

One explanation lies in the very nature of the spirit world and spirit communication. Reported repeatedly through various mediumistic channels and sources is the ability of spirits to use telepathy. Spirits have a sense of *knowing* each other, without having to speak a word. I'm sure that's how I knew it was Jesus. The knowledge was infused into me—my consciousness enveloped by the consciousness of Jesus. At one point in my sketchbook I actually wrote: "I am Jesus."

Jesus was confirming who he was and showing me a sample of how automatic writing worked—six years before I was introduced to the messages from Jesus through Padgett. And the Holy Spirit was there, imparting God's blessings of Love.

But this was very confusing because of what I had read about reincarnation. *Did this mean I was the reincarnation of Jesus?* I questioned this because I was not perfect, and I knew I was certainly *not* qualified to be his Second Coming! I had been a sinner, but Jesus assured me that it didn't matter to God. He would still give me His Love, and I could embody the Christ consciousness, like Jesus.

Imagine my husband's shock when he came home and I told him about my visit from Jesus! To his credit, he did not try to take me to another psychiatrist, or to the psych hospital. It took years to come to a sensible understanding of that experience, even though I had been acquainted with the spirit world since childhood. If only we had known about the Padgett messages, it would've saved us so much grief and confusion.

We would have immediately understood that I had been blessed to receive a call from Jesus and that I was in such close rapport with him that it *felt* like I was him. *Not* that I *was* Jesus. But this is what being in rapport is like. It can make you feel as if you *are* that person.

———✳———

CHAPTER 7

CONFIRMATIONS & CHANNELING

"Confirmations may come in many forms and at any time."

—Aleksandra Layland, engineer and author

AS A DISCERNING individual I was curious to see how others had reacted to the Padgett messages. I began a relentless pursuit to find out everything I could about these writings and their integration into the world.

Dozens of books and websites are available now about the messages. Thirty years ago, I could find only two outside sources: Brad Steiger's *Revelation: The Divine Fire: An Investigation of Men and Women Who Claim to be in Spiritual Communication with a Higher Intelligence*, and Jon Klimo's *Channeling*.

The Divine Fire

In *Revelation: The Divine Fire,* Brad Steiger, an independent investigator of the paranormal, makes an inquiry into the universal principles underlying the spiritual experience of transformation. In the introduction, he calls upon Paul's conversion on the road to Damascus to point out that this change can occur in an instant. He compares this to many similar modern-day reports. "Where better to seek a description of the Face of God than in an examination of the lives and the testimony of those who have been consumed by the Divine Fire?" (Steiger, 1973: 17)

Steiger's first chapter deals with the fundamentalist attitude toward new revelation. Their predominant view is, if it's not in the Bible, it's not worth paying attention to. Steiger points to how fundamentalist Christians use Galatians 1:8 as a proof text that warns against adding to or taking away from the Bible in any way. "But even if we or an angel from heaven should proclaim to you a gospel contrary to what we proclaimed to you, let that one be accursed!" But, the reference in this passage is that the *message* of Jesus, the *gospel,* is the *good news* of Jesus' teachings, *not* what was written about it. (Gospel literally means "good news" in Greek.)

"Revelation as an avenue to knowledge is vastly neglected by both science and religion," stated theologian Bruce Wrightsman. (Steiger, 1973: 33) He says you cannot approach religious experience or knowledge of God without revelation. Most theologians give it a lot of lip service, but seldom take it seriously as a pre-condition. He boldly states: "I think you can make a case for saying all knowledge comes by way of revelation... As far as Divine Revelation is concerned, from my Christian point of view, it's undeniable. I see too many evidences of it around, too many experiences of it in my own life." (Steiger, 1973: 33)

So many people have been consumed by the *Divine Fire* and compelled to speak out about it, that Steiger finds it difficult to believe "that any one religious body might have cornered the market." (Steiger, 1973: 39) He further states that many contemporary revelators report that the Bible does, indeed, need supplements.

It is in this context that Steiger introduces James Padgett and the messages he received through automatic writings. After investigating many revelations, including the Seth writings and Edgar Cayce material, Steiger focuses on the Padgett messages in his chapter entitled "New Gospels for a New Age." He devotes over two-thirds of the chapter to quoting messages from Jesus, Mary, John of Patmos, John the disciple of Jesus, and Paul.

The Padgett messages play a vital role in his book. Even though he goes on to report other examples of experiences with the *Divine Fire*, to no other movement or individual does he give more attention than the Padgett messages. In Chapter 11, "Judgment Day Isn't What It Used to Be," he again turns to the Padgett messages for enlightenment on this subject, by quoting a message from Jesus on "The Great Day of Judgment." It is clear that Steiger was impressed with Padgett's automatic writings and made them a crucial part of his book, viewed in a highly positive light.

Channeling

The second source mentioning the Padgett messages was Jon Klimo's *Channeling: Investigations on Receiving Information from Paranormal Sources.* A survey and source book, it is considered to be *the* definitive work on all facets of channeling. It gives a historical look from the earliest recorded instance up to the date of the book's publication in 1987. Klimo is a professor at The American Schools of Professional

Psychology, a graduate school of Argosy University in the San Francisco Bay area. He devotes a paragraph to the Padgett messages:

> James E. Padgett was a conscientious, analytical Vermont lawyer for thirty-five years before reluctantly claiming to receive messages from spirits for the last eight years of his life (he died in 1923). For a long time, Padgett wrote, he refused to believe the sources were who they claimed to be, especially Jesus. But eventually he reached the point where he could say, 'I believe in the truth of these communications with as little doubt as I ever believed in the truth of a fact established by the most positive evidence in court.' The work became documented in the multivolumed *True Gospel Revealed Anew by Jesus*. (Klimo, 1987: 109)

Though it may be a small reference, he characterizes Padgett as conscientious and analytical. He emphasizes Padgett's own reluctance to believe what was being channeled through him, and his reluctance to make claims about it, but he did finally come to believe.

The content of channeled material must stand on its own merits. No matter where the material comes from, we must analyze it for ourselves, using our reason and intuition. The value of the material can, and should, be established through personal experience. (Klimo, 1987) Klimo writes that throughout history, channeled material tends to fall into the following categories:

- Ageless wisdom
- Guidance for daily living and other personal messages
- Various "proof" from the sources
- Descriptions of the realities experienced by the sources
- Information about the past and future
- Subject matter for artistic and creative expression

- Scientific, technological, and medical/healing information (Klimo, 1987)

One of the most important aims of channeling, asserts Klimo, is to provide proof of survival after death. One form of proof is for the channeled entities to provide clues—like a pet name used by a spouse, the location of lost personal items, or descriptions of events known only to the surviving spouse. This is what Helen, Padgett's wife, did to convince him that she was writing through him.

A leading explanation by skeptics is that the channel picks up relevant information through unconscious telepathy from the minds of other people present, usually the one seeking contact with the deceased. But Klimo points out that there are many cases where it is hard to maintain this view.

Proof of Spirit Contact

Forms of proof cited by Klimo include the use of codes, book tests, cross-correspondences, and word-association tests. The magician Harry Houdini proved to be an excellent example of the use of codes. Before he died, Houdini and his wife agreed on a ten-word secret code that he thought would provide proof of continuation after death, if he could get the message to her after he died. In February, 1928, after Houdini's death, he transmitted the following message through the trance medium Arthur Ford (Mrs. Houdini was *not* present at this sitting):

> A man who says he is Harry Houdini... is here and wishes to send his wife, Beatrice Houdini, the ten-word code which he agreed to do if it were possible for him to communicate. He says you are to take this message to her upon acceptance

of it, he wishes her to follow out the plan they agreed upon before his passing. This is the code: "ROSABELLE** ANSWER** TELL** PRAY** ANSWER** ANSWER** TELL** ANSWER** ANSWER** TELL"… He says the code is known only to him and to his wife, and that no one on earth but those two know it. (Klimo, 1987: 154-155)

Ford delivered the message immediately to Mrs. Houdini, who confirmed the words. Ford re-entered the trance state and channeled a series of further codes between Houdini and his wife, including the intricacies of their code that involved certain letters in the earlier ten-word passage.

Mrs. Houdini was very moved by the experience. Harry Houdini himself was excited as he channeled through Ford:

Tell the whole world that Harry Houdini still lives and will prove it a thousand times and more…. I was perfectly honest and sincere in trying to disprove survival, though I resorted to tricks to prove my point for the simple reason that I did not believe communication was true, but I did no more than seemed justifiable. I am now sincere in sending this through in my desire to undo. Tell all those who lost faith because of my mistake to lay hold again of hope, and to live with the knowledge that life is continuous. This is my message to the world, through my wife and through this instrument. (Klimo, 1987: 155)

The cross-correspondence method of proving survival was invented by F.W.H. Myers, the noted nineteenth century British poet, essayist and founder of the Society for Psychical Research. This method has been widely used to show that channeling connects people with the dead. This approach is convincing to critics who claim the material is being drawn from the medium's own subliminal mind or derived by telepathic means from people there.

Klimo cites a comprehensive set of cross-correspondence recorded at the British Society of Psychical Research in Cambridge. Myers himself, who died in 1901, and others, communicated through four different mediums in England, and other channels in Europe and the U.S. during a forty-year period. Intricate webs of information from the same sources to the different channels provide powerful arguments for spirit communication through channeling. (Klimo, 1987: 156)

Carl Jung provides an example of a book test in a spontaneous, clairvoyant channeling episode. He was lying awake thinking of the sudden death of a friend whose funeral had been the day before. Suddenly he felt as if his friend was in the room, standing at the foot of the bed, asking him to go with him. Jung followed in his imagination: "He led me… to his house… He climbed on a stool and showed me the second of five books with red bindings which stood on the second shelf from the top."

The next morning, he went to his friend's widow and asked whether he could look up something in his friend's library. "Sure enough, there was a stool standing under the bookcase I had seen in my vision, and even before I came closer, I could see the five books with red bindings… The title of the second volume read: *The Legacy of the Dead*." (Klimo 1987: 156-157)

Psychological word-association tests designed by Carl Jung also provided evidence that the entities were who they said they were. Jung's idea was that certain tests could be used to draw out material that was unique to the discarnate human spirits, and that the personalities of sources could be identified. (Klimo, 1987)

Applying the rationale of this test, consider the following excerpt of a letter from Jesus to Padgett: "You are in me and I am in thee, and we are in the Father. You are in me for all eternity… My kingdom is not of this world and you are not of this world—you are in me as I told my disciples of old. Only believe me and keep my commandments, and I will love you to the end, and the Father will love you." (Padgett, 1958: II:23)

This sounds like the same Jesus in John 17:21: "… that they may all be one. As you, Father, are in me and I am in you, may they also be in us, so that the world may believe that you have sent me and have loved them even as you have loved me." And John 18:36: "My kingdom is not from this world."

In another example from the Padgett messages, Jesus states: "I am the vine and you are the branch." (Padgett, 1958: II:24) John 15:5 reports Jesus as saying: "I am the vine, you are the branches."

Klimo describes channeling primarily as an *identity* (the source), separate from the channel, who exercises *control* over the motor, perceptual or cognitive abilities of the medium, once the medium relinquishes control. He clarifies the distinction between two basic kinds of channeling: *intentional* and *spontaneous*:

> In intentional channeling, the person who is channeling controls the phenomenon and can usually produce it at will, or is at least a willing participant. In spontaneous channeling… the individual is not able to control the activity and is at the mercy of its comings and goings. Spontaneous channeling has an unbidden, intrusive quality; those who prize personal autonomy and control see it as a violation of the individual's integrity by uncontrollable forces. In some cases, however, the spontaneous channel does want the contact but is unable to control its form or timing. (Klimo, 1987: 185-186)

Different Forms of Channeling

Professor Klimo also makes an important distinction between *mental* and *physical* channeling:

> *Mental* channeling involves mediating information—thoughts, words, images, and feelings. In *physical* channeling on the other hand, the channel (or the source) affects the physical environment in some way. This may involve healing of the physical body, materialization, or the bending or movement of an object. Cases of this kind are far more rare than the mental kind. (Klimo, 1987: 185-186)

Various forms of channeling, covered in great detail by Klimo, include full trance, sleep, dream, light trance, clairaudient, clairvoyant, automatisms, and open channeling. Automatic writing, related to full-trance and light-trance channeling, merits its own category. It has a dissociated quality unique to it. Hundreds of published accounts reveal a channel being aware and awake...but separated from any sense of controlling the writing, appearing to have his arm and hand controlled by another:

> The chief characteristic of this phenomenon is that it is an *automatism*—that is, the motor activity involved with the writing occurs automatically and unconsciously, with no intentional control exercised by the channel.... Although the automatic writer is unconscious with regard to the activity of part of the body, the mind is otherwise clear and alert. (Klimo, 1987: 196)

The Padgett messages relate the following description of how the spirits controlled his writing, *not* Padgett: "The communications that you receive as to these truths are written by us and in our own words ... your mind does not supply a thought or suggestion ... you are used only as a medium to convey our thoughts, and lend your physical organs to facilitate our expressing in our own language the truths that we desire to convey." (Padgett, 1958: I:339)

Discernment

All channels and their sources say *discernment* is crucial. Klimo asserts "if channeling distinct entity-type personalities is involved we... need to discern the nature, quality, and trustworthiness of the source." He quotes the entity *Lazaris*, through channel Jach Pursel, and makes an excellent point about discernment: "People assume that if it's a channeled entity then it's got to be speaking the ... highest truth ... [but] there are good entities and bad entities, as far as the quality of information goes." Professor Klimo expounds:

> We must guard against the charisma of authority. As you have heard numerous times before, just because we may believe that information comes from some glamorous paranormal source, we should not fail to scrutinize its content and weigh our response to it as carefully as if it came from...a workshop leader or university lecturer. (Klimo, 1987: 322-323)

The entity *Lazaris* suggested scrutinizing the messages from himself and other sources by applying the following questions:

> First, are the teachings limited? Are the teachings giving you the sense that you are less than you are? Second, can I apply

this? Can I use this? What's it going to do for me? Third, as I apply what's being said, am I happier? Am I more myself and is my life working better? Fourth, when I come away from the experience, am I feeling and am I thinking more positively? (Klimo, 1987: 323)

Echoing speculations by skeptics about the authenticity of channeled material, Alice Bailey channeled the following from her source, *The Tibetan*: "Two percent of the material purported to be channeled comes from 'masters' to their disciples; 5 percent is from more advanced disciples in training on the inner planes; 8 percent is from the channels' own higher Selves or souls; and some 85 percent is from the personal subconscious of the channels." (Klimo, 1987: 321)

Klimo points out that experienced channeling teachers are the first to affirm that most alleged channeling is instead "the product of self-delusion brought on as a result of psychic immaturity. Or, through a kind of self-hypnosis, some so-called channeling is simply imagination creating its own characters." (Klimo, 1987: 321)

After fifty years of researching this medium of communication, and having experienced channeling myself, I agree that a small percentage of this material comes from spirit entities. The great majority comes from the unconscious mind, is imagination, or outright fraud. Unfortunately, many critics refuse to see beyond the many frauds. But the skeptics who do, end up becoming convinced of the reality of the spirit world and spirit communication.

———✸———

"If our ideas are not evolving with verifiable evidence, they are not reliable ideas."

—Carmine Savastano, author and speaker

Appointment to President of the Foundation

"Once we make our decision, all things will come to us. Auspicious signs are not a superstition, but a confirmation. They are a response."

—Deng Ming-Dao, artist and Taoist author, b. 1954

Our vision quest destination was Santa Cruz, California. It was early September, 1983. My husband, Jonathan, and I, were seeking inspiration and support from Bill Asnis, a Foundation minister. We aspired to become ministers and establish a Foundation branch in our area of North County San Diego.

On the drive back home, we received some odd guidance. For no apparent reason, we were impressed that a change in leadership in the Foundation would be corroborated by three separate mediums. This was puzzling because we were not part of the leadership. We were not even ministers yet.

Days after returning home, Bill called to tell us the new president of the Foundation, Victor Summers, was moving the organization to our area. With great excitement, we wrote to inquire how we could help. We had written a month earlier about our desire to help spread the message about Jesus' teachings through Padgett. We communicated our intent to develop a branch in San Diego and about a *Divine Love Uprising* celebration and retreat that we intended to host.

Soon after, we received a phone call from Victor, informing us that he and some other members of the Foundation were in Crest, California, only an hour from where we lived in North County San Diego. We arranged a meeting and immediately became immersed in Foundation activities.

One evening, after we had been dancing and praising God, I was standing next to Victor when I became aware of Jesus standing next to me, his arm around me. I was in awe and ecstatic, and suddenly I found myself on the floor, *slain in the spirit* from the power of the Love! It was astounding! I did not feel myself go to the floor, or land, and I was not hurt in the least.

A few months later, Victor, conflicted and overwhelmed with his responsibilities, departed for Florida and left the Foundation materials in our care. Then, on March 31, 1984, Victor called us from Florida, stating that he had received guidance from Jesus that I was to be president of the Foundation, and Jonathan was to be vice president. During the call, Jonathan and I received a powerful inflowing of Divine Love, giving us corroboration of God's blessings. Honored, we accepted the invitation.

During the next few days, another confirmation came through Carolyn Bowman, a Divine Love medium who had come across the country with Victor. This was the third medium to verify my appointment to the presidency (Victor Summers, Jonathan Sperry, and Carolyn Bowman).

Three days later, on April 3, 1984, more validation came from Jesus and the Padgetts. *Simultaneously*, while Jonathan and I faced one another, we received an anointing of God's Love, along with the vision of the spirits of James and Helen Padgett, hovering over us both. Then the spirit of Jesus came and hovered over all four of us. It was rapturous! It seemed as if we were entering the gateway to Heaven.

———— ✳ ————

Excerpts from *Declaration of Jonathan Alfred Sperry*:

On March 31st, 1984, my wife, Patricia Sperry, and I, Jonathan Sperry, received a telephone call from Victor Summers, Chief Elder and President of the Foundation Church of the New Birth, who was in Florida at the time, stating that Jesus had come to him with the desire that Patricia Sperry take full material responsibility for the Foundation Church of the New Birth as its new President and that I was to be Vice President and Patricia's partner in this responsibility. At the time, Patricia was serving as Corporate Secretary of the Church, which appointment was also bestowed by Victor Summers under Jesus' guidance. During this telephone conversation of March 31st, I was sitting close to Patricia and we went into a deep state of prayer, seeking for greater understanding and corroboration, when we felt an unquestionable blessing and anointing of God's Love, accompanied by the presence of Celestial Spirits.

A series of powerful spiritual experiences and inflowings of God's Divine Love followed in the days to come, culminating, on the evening of April 3rd, 1984, in an experience in which we were lifted into an altered, trance-like state, far above our normal levels of perception. It felt as though a veil had been parted and we could see clearly with our spiritual vision Helen and James Padgett coming over Patricia and myself, respectively, and engulfing us in their intense love. We then felt the awesome presence of Jesus, who gently swooped down and engulfed the four of us with his love, as we felt yet another anointing of God's Love. This blessing totally amazed us in that we had *both* experienced and saw the same vision simultaneously.

These events, along with other experiences, circumstances, and corroborations occurring both before and after Victor's call, led us to believe beyond any shadow of a doubt, that we were being called to take on the important and sacred responsibility of the protection and care of the Foundation Church of the New Birth (Mother Church), which included trusteeship of the fragile original Padgett messages, at that very urgent and precarious time in the Church's history.... Patricia and I chose to accept what we felt was the Will of God and in April of 1984 we negotiated and signed a new lease for the Crest home and assumed our spiritual and physical responsibilities to the best of our abilities and resources, having faith in God's Love and care....

Being trustees to these sacred documents is not a responsibility that we have ever taken lightly, nor have we been motivated by any personal glory or prestige, but only have in our minds and hearts the desire to do what is best for the messages....

[We] have, truly, completely dedicated our entire lives, energy, resources, and talents to this great work of spreading the Padgett messages and showing forth God's Divine Love in whatever ways we can, and consider this to be a great blessing and honor, and would do so regardless of any church materials or organization entrusted to our care. Our desire and prayer is that we can all come into harmony at this time so that the important work of enlightening the world as to the existence of the messages from Jesus and the Angels and the availability of the Divine Love can be amplified and unity can be achieved among the brothers and sisters in this work.

I do hereby testify that these are the facts as they unfolded.

Signed and dated December 31, 1985   Jonathan Alfred Sperry

You may find it curious that there are two organizations with the same name, Foundation Church of the New Birth (FCNB). The *Reformed* FCNB, currently located in Williamsville, New York, came into existence in 1991 when some members broke off from the Foundation

Church of Divine Truth (FCDT). The FCDT formed in the mid-1980s, after the Padgett messages went into public domain. (Copyright law put the messages into the public domain in 1984, sixty years after James Padgett's death in 1924.) The *Reformed* FCNB decided to use the same name, even though the by-laws they adopted are completely different than the *original* FCNB's.

Each organization is separate and sovereign. Neither has authority over the other. It is beneficial for both entities to exist. Wouldn't Jesus and his colleagues encourage all efforts to bring these messages to the awareness of more people? Ultimately, we have the same purpose of spreading Jesus' messages about God's Love, through dissemination and preservation of the automatic writings received through James Padgett.

I prefer to refer to the *original* FCNB as the "Foundation," as I have throughout this book, because Divine Love is the foundation we all stand on. It also helps to avoid some confusion because the FCNB is *not* a fundamentalist Christian church—"New Birth" in the title is *not* synonymous with fundamentalism's "born again" doctrine. It is not even a traditional church. The organization was founded in 1958 to preserve, publish and disseminate the messages from Jesus and other Celestials through James Padgett.

————>|<————

CHAPTER 8

A SPIRITUAL CRUCIBLE

"The fact that an opinion has been widely held is no evidence whatever that it is not utterly absurd."

—Bertrand Russell, Nobel laureate philosopher and author, b. 1872

"In searching out the truth be ready for the unexpected, for it is difficult to find and puzzling when you find it."

—Heraclitus, pre-Socratic Greek philosopher, b. 535 B.C.

JIM JONES PROMISED his followers an Eden in the jungles of Gyana in Jonestown, but on November 18, 1978, it all ended in the most horrific forced mass-suicide imaginable. Nine hundred and nine people, a third of them children, drank a grape-flavored liquid laced with cyanide, knowing it would result in death. Well, the adults knew, but many of the children given the drink by their parents didn't know. Their parents' thinking had become deranged by blindly following a cult leader, who was actually deluded and crazed from rampant drug abuse. The phrase "drinking the Kool-Aid," referring to followership at its most extreme, was coined after this massacre.

Another wake-up call to the extreme danger of deranged religious thinking comes from the Waco massacre, which ended in a fiery fulfillment of the expectations of self-proclaimed prophet David Koresh. Koresh took over a heretical sect of former Seventh-Day Adventists and turned it into a personal cult of Branch Davidians in Waco, Texas. He claimed to be a prophet king and a warrior angel with the keys to heaven. Koresh taught a strong apocalyptic religious message with emphasis on a holy war provoked by an oppressive government. They believed the American army would attack and bring about the end of the world. *Their* world came to an end, as expected, on April 19, 1993, after a 51-day standoff with federal ATF agents and the U.S. military. They expected a fiery end, and they got it. Eighty-two people passed into the afterlife during the siege, including twenty children.

The Jonestown and Waco tragedies show that it is not sensible to surrender the rational mind in the hope of a promised transcendental utopia. And watch out for apocalyptic self-proclaimed "prophets." Spiritual seekers are now developing a keener sense of discrimination, and rightly so. Many gurus and movements have been exposed for unethical and illegal acts—egotistical power plays, violent retaliations against detractors, sexual misconduct, mass suicide, and murder.

David Christopher Lane, professor of philosophy and sociology at Mt. San Antonio College in Walnut, CA, and editor of *Understanding Cults and New Religions,* presents a useful set of criteria in his article "The Spiritual Crucible: A Critical Guide to America's Religious/

Cultic Renaissance." Lane poses crucial questions that arise in judging the authenticity of channeled material, teachers, or movements:

> If the teachings don't make logical sense on this plane, what is the assurance that they will come together in the higher astral worlds? Why does my teacher have the privilege to rationalize away his worldly expressions of anger and lust, as part of his awakening method, when my same actions are always called vices to be conquered? Is the thinking mind really the enemy that should be suppressed and fought? (Lane, 1986: 78-79)

Serious religious seekers who are not satisfied with dogmatic and fundamentalist perspectives argue that if one is striving for an enlightened state, then *all* parts of his being should reflect that truth: soul, mind, and body. "To castrate the one versus the other," Lane proclaims, "is to allow for only a schizophrenic view of the universe. That is, the body is *always* evil; and the soul *always* good. God, in the meantime, ceases to be the Lord of all and becomes the Chosen God of the few." (Lane, 1986: 79)

Many sincere seekers overcome this dualism by using reason to *aid* and *promote* spiritual practice. Analytical intelligence is not a hindrance in the soul's progression to God, but a vital and valuable step. To deny reasoning and its importance is not progressive, but a regression into intellectual infancy. Although few in number, true saints and masters do not ask for blind obedience, but instead stress individuality and responsibility. "Unlike their charlatan counterparts," says Lane, "genuine masters invite critical thinking.... But how does one know if his spiritual master is authentic or misguided? How can one distinguish between a legitimate and beneficial path and a self-serving and corrupt organization?" (Lane, 1986: 79)

Lane clarifies many issues facing the spiritual community. He offers a *crucible* with a series of key questions, each designed to discern the credibility of one's chosen teacher or path. It is based on criteria suggested by four distinct schools of both Eastern and Western spiritual traditions, even though they may not agree with each other.

Together, these traditions provide a comprehensive template, and serve to avoid the ethnocentrism implicit in the guidelines proposed by almost all religious groups. Lane points out that no critical guide is exempt from some bias. But it can be minimized if the model used for assessment is interdisciplinary and drawn from cross-cultural sources. Due to their unique distinctions, the primary sources employed by Lane are:

- **Transpersonal Psychology**—the "spiritual" branch of psychology that integrates spiritual and transcendent aspects of the human experience; based on the principles of Carl Jung, Abraham Maslow and William James.
- **Sant Mat**—a spiritual movement with beginnings in thirteenth century CE India; based on the teachings of Hindu mystical saints.
- **Advaita Vedanta**—a branch of Hinduism founded by Adi Shankara (700-750 CE); based on classical sacred Hindu texts.
- **Christianity**—the world's most prevalent religion with two thousand years of history; based on the life and teachings of Jesus of Nazareth.

Lane's spiritual crucible is comprised of seven questions.

1. Is There a Charge for Membership?

Lane begins by quoting Julian P. Johnson from *The Path of the Masters* (1939):

Real masters never charge for their services, nor do they accept payment in any form… This is a universal law among Masters, and yet it is an amazing fact that thousands of eager seekers in America and elsewhere, go on paying large sums of money for 'spiritual instruction.' Masters are always self-sustaining. They are never supported by their students or by public charity. (Lane, 1986: 80)

Groups that require money for their teachings should be suspect. Lane acknowledges that money is necessary for the publishing of books and publications to keep the movement functioning. He states, "there is a distinct line between obligatory payments—even if disguised as 'love offerings'—and unsolicited donations; the latter have justifiable reasons behind them, whereas the former makes religion a business enterprise, with a very lucrative tax shelter." (Lane, 1986: 80)

He further reports that there are few spiritual groups that do *not* charge money for membership, so this question is a good way to discern a genuine path from one less valid. If money is collected, to whom does it go and for what purpose? If there is resistance to giving out financial information, then proceed *very* cautiously, if at all.

2. Does Your Spiritual Teacher Embody High Ethics?

A true enlightened master exhibits the highest ethical qualities, like honesty, kindness, integrity, and charity, by virtue of being connected to God.

"Let's be frank, Lane says, "no other field attracts more cranks and charlatans than religion. Yet, in spite of this, there is very little critical discrimination among religious devotees." (Lane, 1986: 89) Instead, gullible followers resort to mind-numbing irrationalities: "Well, my guru is beyond good and bad, so whatever he does is for the best." With this mistaken logic, a spiritual leader could justify any action whatsoever. A following that placed him beyond reproach enabled Jim Jones to be the leader of over nine hundred cult suicides in Jonestown. Gurus don't hesitate to point out their devotees' weaknesses, Lane says, so disciples should not be hesitant to criticize their teacher's faults when they appear: "Critical exchange is crucial and healthy for any type of relationship—including teacher/student ones." (Lane 1986: 82)

Lane asserts, however, that no human being is perfect: "A perfect master is not one with a perfect body or mind, but a person who realizes fully that all bodies or manifestations are destined to die—including his own—and surrenders to a Reality *greater* than himself." (Lane, 1986: 89)

3. Does Your Master Make Claims About His Spiritual Development, Powers, or Attainment?

It is almost universally proclaimed in the world's great religious scriptures that humility is a prime virtue of an enlightened master. Yet many teachers boast of their spiritual attainments, sometimes to the extreme of claiming to be God incarnated. In 1986, there were over a *million* gurus in India, most claiming "direct contact with the highest Reality and Truth." (Lane, 1986) Lane says not to *believe* any of it, but to trust only your own experience:

> Spirituality, according to true mystics of all ages, is an experiential science, one which demands not blind faith and belief, but rigorous practice and application…. Therefore, the necessity for "belief" in a teacher's claims is uncalled for. Rather, what *is* needed is experimental verification of the path he/she advocates…. If any guru demands belief in his/her status it is obvious that what they are teaching is *not* spirituality/mysticism but dogma and conversion. (Lane, 1986: 83)

Saints from different cultures throughout the ages have realized the highest qualities of spiritual awareness in their everyday lives. They serve as reference points for modern seekers to measure the claims of spiritual leaders. Rare twentieth century examples are Paramahansa Yogananda, Ramana Maharshi, Sawan Singh, and Mother Theresa.

4. Does Your Group Proselytize Vigorously for New Converts?

Any group that fervently emphasizes proselytizing is a dividing force in relationships and families. A conversionary force tends to create dualistic factions where none had before existed. Obvious examples from fundamentalist Christian and Islamic sects are: *I am saved; you are lost. I found it; you haven't.* Subtle examples come from Scientology (*Are you clear?*) and other esoteric groups that have "initiated" members versus "non-initiated."

Every religious movement has some form of advertising, the most benign being the publication of books, texts, and articles. But there is a difference between *giving* out the message and *pushing* the truth as a required necessity. Rather than a free-will choice.

The trouble with pushy exclusiveness is that if you have *the* way, then you can justify virtually *any* means. Including "holy war," which then isn't considered a sin or murder because the people you are killing aren't considered people, but infidels.

"If the guru/path really does have a glimpse into the transcendental truth of the universe, says Lane, "then the concern will not be with *preaching* that insight but actually exemplifying it." (Lane, 1986: 84) The best teacher is one who speaks actions, not words.

5. Who Appointed Your Teacher a Master? What Is the Historical Tradition Behind the Movement?

Watch out for self-proclaimed charismatic prophets. When doubt surfaces with questions like, "*Is my guru really enlightened? Did my teacher truly receive the mantleship from his master? Why is my movement's history disputed by outside scholars?"*, the remedy to this doubt is *not* blind faith, but to allow the mind to question—to exist in harmony with the devotional heart, and seek answers. Lane states:

> This is the human dilemma: we can *never* know anything, including God, in its entirety.... The mind is simply incapable of understanding that which ultimately transcends it entirely. Thus, genuine spiritual practice does not try to squelch the mind, but only understands its limitations. (Lane, 1986: 85)

Certain requirements must be met before the seeker can feel comfortable. The history of the group should be studied for intellectual soundness. The teacher must have verification by *outside* sources. Otherwise, if *only* the teacher is able to verify his realizations, all kinds of problems may arise, including the self-appointment of the teacher as the final and only authority.

The world's great religious traditions have lines of transference, testing, and corroborating a person's qualifications. This serves as a "quality control" to make sure that a teacher doesn't distort the teachings for personal gain. Lane cites Paul Twitchell as an example of a spiritual teacher without any historical roots. Twitchell made up almost all his claims to mastership and the traditions of his group, Eckankar. He stole most of his writings from other authors, including Julian P. Johnson's books from the 1930s.

6. Are the Central Teachings Trans-rational or Pre-rational?

Trans-rational disciplines focus on higher states of consciousness beyond the verbal mind. They help you master the lower habits of the mind. *Trans*-rational thinking does not exclude analytical thinking. But it helps the process by acknowledging the potential of human existence.

Pre-rational thinking includes dogma, groupthink, mythic logic, and obedience without insight. These behaviors do not promote spiritual attainment, but work *against* it. The Jim Jones cult is an example of *pre*-rational thinking. The members gave up their individuality for "regressive magical-mythic belonging." (Lane, 1986: 86)

An authentic tradition or religion emphasizes direct, *personal* contact with God by practicing daily meditation and prayer, *trans*-rational activities where your intelligence stays with you. "Nothing can substitute for the disciple's own effort and inward progress—not vicarious atonement, not the burning of karmas by the guru, not God's grace, though all of these elements have their part," writes Lane. He goes on to state: "No true mystic will ever ask a student to believe in him blindly or follow the teachings uncritically." (Lane, 1986: 86)

Lane quotes examples from the Sant Mat tradition (*When with my own eyes do I behold, then shall I accept what the Sat-Guru saith*), and Sikhism (*Until with my own eyes do I see, the word of the guru satisfieth me not*). Don't drink the Kool-Aid.

7. What Are the Daily Results of Your Interaction with the Teachings?

Loyalty to your spiritual path should result in a noticeable difference in kindness, compassion, honesty, openness, selflessness, and loving devotion. If not, then either you are not consistently practicing the teachings, or you may be following a path which places more emphasis on pre-rational, self-centered, and antisocial behavior. If the path is genuine, it will help you better understand yourself, your relationships, and God, even though your worldly life may not get better. "Following a spiritual path does not insure one against losing money, facing natural catastrophes, and struggling with domestic problems," states Lane. "It only helps one in coping better with all the various aspects of human existence. There is as much responsibility on the shoulders of a disciple as there is on a guru. Both must be willing to surrender to a reality higher than themselves." (Lane, 1986: 87)

If you find that your teacher charges for membership, proclaims his own mastership, claims to be God-incarnated, requires complete compliance, emphasizes proselytizing, encourages pre-rational thinking, and lives an unethical lifestyle, then assume your teacher is not genuine.

On the other hand, Lane says if your teacher or path "scores positively in all areas (such an accomplishment, by the way, is rare), then you are very fortunate to have been led to a beneficial and legitimate spiritual movement." Your responsibility then is to claim the blessing. "Enlightenment is a two way process," states Lane, "the outcome of two interacting forces: God's grace and the disciple's efforts." (Lane, 1986: 88)

Lane acknowledges that most of the results will be a mix of positive and negative scores. It is essential that the seeker weigh the pros and cons. If you stay with the teachings, discard what is not in your best interest. If you leave, take the beneficial aspects with you. Lane concludes:

> Following a spiritual master or path requires a tremendous amount of maturity, self-control, and discrimination. To achieve God-Realization is not an overnight affair, or the outcome of feeble effort; it is the culmination of consistent day to day application of transcendent mystical teachings. (Lane, 1986: 88)

We must never let others do our thinking for us. We must examine any new ideology or revelation with critical, skeptical, open eyes.

Here is how the Padgett messages fare in Lane's crucible:

1. Is There a Charge for Membership?

James Padgett never practiced mediumship for money. Books and printed materials are sold, but are also often given out for free. There is no charge for membership. Donations are accepted, but not solicited.

2. Does Your Spiritual Teacher Embody High Ethics?

I have been involved in the leadership of the Foundation since 1984, including being a trustee for many of the archival materials. I have never encountered any material about Padgett that would cast a questionable light on his character. I have seen no evidence of any accusations of illegal or improper conduct on Padgett's part.

3. Claims About Spiritual Attainment or Powers:

James Padgett was a private person who never made public claims about his spiritual development or powers. He had many doubts and questions about the phenomenon happening through him. The following letter to Dr. George H. Gilbert, dated December 28, 1915, is revealing:

> First permit me to state that I am a practical lawyer of 35 years experience and as such not inclined to accept allegations of fact as true without evidencing proof. I was born and reared in an orthodox Protestant church and until quite recently remained orthodox in my beliefs; that a little more than a year ago, upon the suggestion being made to me that I was a psychic, I commenced to receive by way of automatic writing messages from what was said to be messages from the spirit world and since that time I have received nearly 1500 such messages upon many subjects but mostly as to things of a

spiritual and religious nature, not orthodox, as to the errancy of the Bible.

I have not space to name nor would you probably be interested in the great number of the writers of these messages, but among the writers is Jesus of Nazareth, from whom I have received more than 100 messages. I will frankly say, that I refused for a long time to believe that these messages came from Jesus, because God, while He had the power as I believed, would not engage in doing such a thing. But the evidence of the truth of the origin of these messages became so convincing not only from the great number and positiveness of the witnesses, but from the inherent and unusual merits of the contents of the messages that I was forced to believe, and now say to you that I believe in the truth of these communications with as little doubt as I ever believed in the truth of a fact established by the most positive evidence in court. I wish further to say, that to my own consciousness I did no thinking in writing the messages. I did not know what was to be written nor what was written at the time except the word that the pencil was writing. (Padgett, 1958: I:3-4)

Padgett never claimed to be God. In the messages from Jesus, not even Jesus claimed to be God, but instead makes a strong point of denying that he is God.

In my teachings I want to show that I am only my Father's son as you are His son, and not to be worshiped as God. He is the only God and the people who are worshiping me in all parts of the world are not doing what I desire, for they are putting God in the background and making me their object of worship, which is all wrong and which I am so anxious to have ceased.... They must look upon me only as a son of God and their elder brother who has received from the Father His full Love and confidence, and which I am bidden to teach to them. You are not to let anyone tempt you to let your love of God be displaced by any love that you may have for me, for your love for me must not be the kind that you have for Him. He is the only God and you must worship Him alone. So be careful and make the distinction, or you will make a most egregious mistake. (Padgett, 1958: I:XIII)

If Padgett were a fake, he wouldn't write this. It went against his orthodox religious beliefs that Jesus was God. Padgett stated to his friend, Dr. Leslie Stone (a witness to the development of his mediumship and present when Padgett received automatic writings), that his "conception of religious doctrine was simply that which emanated from" the "Trinity Methodist Church in Washington D.C.," where he taught Sunday School for many years. He was also a practicing lawyer for more than four decades, a man in his golden years who was not looking for a following. He did not try to impress any crowds, and he had nothing to gain from this. If anything, he stood to lose credibility and standing in the community, especially the orthodox religious community.

Great emphasis is placed on the experience of being at-one with God. The writings encourage prayer and spiritual development, rather than following any human leader. Jesus is the greatest and most loving of all spirits, but Jesus is not necessary as an intermediary to connect with God. "I, Jesus, as the Son of Man or of God, do not save any man from his sins and make him at-one with the Father, but the truths which I taught, and which were taught me by the Father, are things that save." (Padgett, 1958: I:209) The only way a person can *really* know the truth is to go to God. *True authority* comes from God.

4. Does Your Group Proselytize Vigorously?

The Foundation was established in 1958, based on the messages received by Padgett, thirty-five years after his death. The messages have spread through books, publications, personal testimonies, and individuals being spiritually guided. We don't recruit for new converts. Every faith-based group wants to advance or promote its beliefs, and the Foundation wants to spread the knowledge of these remarkable teachings from Jesus. We may recommend or endorse the messages through our testimonies, but we do not peddle our beliefs in a pushy, manipulative, or forceful manner.

We are not exclusive and isolated from other faiths. Jesus gave instructions to Padgett to visit various churches to develop his soul and integrate into established churches.

5. Appointment of Teacher and Historical Tradition:

Jesus chose Padgett as the medium for his messages. The historical traditions behind this movement encompass both the New Testament and Spiritualism.

Even Padgett had grave doubts about the material coming through him, as we have already seen. He was assured and reassured many times, but never asked to *blindly* believe. This message from Jesus explains:

> ...you let doubt come into your mind, and as a consequence, your soul does not respond, although, strange as it may seem, the Divine Love is there, but when this mental doubt exists, it is as if it were a covering which prevents the existence of the Love in the soul to shine forth and produce the great feeling of happiness and joy which otherwise you might experience. The mental condition of the mortal, undoubtedly has a great influence on the consciousness of the man as to his

possession of this soul development and the Divine Love, and consequently, there will have to be this continuous fight as long as life lasts on earth, between the mental conditions and the soul's consciousness. But as the mental beliefs are brought into harmony with the soul's condition, more and more the fight will grow weaker and less frequent, and it is possible that they will cease altogether, and the mental beliefs become entirely and absolutely... absorbed in the soul's consciousness of its being possessed of this Divine Love of the Father. (Padgett, 1958: I:241)

The Divine Love Movement, as it is called by many who have embraced the Padgett messages, has a short history. The messages are not well known yet. But popularity alone does not lend credibility to a teaching or movement. Jim Jones was popular. His congregations in Ukiah and San Francisco, California numbered in the thousands. Several hundred in that group pioneered their way to Jonestown to eventually meet destruction at the hands of their revered leader.

6. Trans-rational or Pre-rational Central Teachings?

The central teachings coming from the messages are definitely *trans*-rational, *not pre*-rational. Emphasis is placed on the importance of using our God-given faculties of intelligence and reasoning to understand and develop a very personal relationship with our Creator. Luke writes: "There is no truth in all God's universe that man is not invited to search for and understand and possess." (Padgett, 1958: I:80)

The Padgett messages contain uncanny clarity and specific information *not* coming from an impersonal universal principle like the "Akashic records" or "The Ascended Masters," but from *real* individuals. Information about Martin Luther and his teachings, for example, come directly from Martin Luther. And information about Jesus and his teachings come directly from Jesus.

Padgett was often encouraged to pray, think spiritual thoughts, engage in activities that would develop his soul, and raise his state of consciousness so he could receive messages of high quality. This communication from Jesus explains:

> Pray often to the Father so that the love may become more abundant and your soul become permeated with it... until by such thinking your brain may become, as it were, infused with these thoughts and thereby receive those qualities that will make its condition similar to the conditions of the minds of the spirits who may wish to form a union with your brain and convey through it the truths that are waiting to be delivered.... your praying must be more frequent so that the soul may be free... of thoughts not spiritual... You need not wait for occasions or opportunities to formally pray but all during the day and evening let your longings for the love ascend to the Father.... Prayers of this kind ascend to the Father and are heard and answered, and, by a law of your relationship to the Father, affect the qualities of the brain in the way of preparing it for the union with the spiritual thoughts of the spirits who desire to write, as I have stated. Your thoughts of spiritual things or of the truths of the spirit world, as they have already been revealed to you, and especially those which pertain to the love and mercy of the Father, and to His will... affect the qualities of the brain so as to produce the condition which is so necessary for our rapport. (Padgett, 1958: I:2-3)

Padgett's own thoughts were not involved in the writing. His own mind was blank and inactive when his brain was being used as the conduit for spirits to write. Whenever Padgett's thinking entered, the spirits would stop writing until Padgett's mind became inactive again. This is how the spirits maintained precise and exact control over what was written.

When a medium's ego enters in, a dilution takes place, allowing untruth to creep in, or personal convictions, suppositions and biases. It's not about personalities or putting a human leader up on a pedestal. It's about sharing our experience and information about God's Love.

Padgett's intelligence stayed with him. He was conscious of and witnessing what was happening. He possessed the gifts of clairvoyance and clairaudience, which gave him the ability to ask the spirits questions and get written answers. Jesus wrote that because of these abilities, Padgett was the only mortal on earth who had heard his voice.

Testimony from Dr. Leslie Stone points out how the writings coming through Padgett came too rapidly to be his own thoughts:

> At this point I must state that I was very often in Mr. Padgett's room when he was receiving these writings and that I am the eye witness to the formation and development of Mr. Padgett as the medium par excellence through which the truths of the Heavenly Father and of life in the spirit world thus obtained have come to mankind... I was... very often present as he continued to receive these messages. They came in a rapid sweep of connected words that obviously gave no time for thought on the part of the writer and, in fact, he often insisted that he had no clear idea of what his pencil was writing until he read the messages afterwards. It was in this way, then, that he received, from 1914 to 1923, some twenty-five hundred messages, many of them coming, I have not the slightest doubt, from those highest spirits whose signatures were testimony to the personalities they represented. (Padgett, 1958: I:IV-V)

Another compelling fact is that most of the messages were received in the presence of the same witnesses: Dr. Leslie R. Stone, Eugene Morgan, and Dr. Goerger. These witnesses provide important corroboration that Padgett was a genuine medium.

7. Daily Results of Interaction with Teachings:

My near-death experience is a dramatic example of the benefits of God's Love in my life. This Love inspired me to undertake a new purpose and responsibility, which I have tested and questioned intensely for over forty years. My faith, hope, Love, and joy has increased in the process.

> Ask, and it will be given you; seek, and you will find; knock, and it will be opened to you. For every one who asks receives, and he who seeks finds, and to him who knocks it will be opened. What father among you, if his son asks for a fish, will instead of a fish give him a serpent; or if he asks for an egg, will give him a scorpion? If you then... know how to give good gifts to your children, how much more will the heavenly Father give the Holy Spirit to those who ask him! (Luke 11:9-13)

———※———

CHAPTER 9

WHAT WOULD JESUS SAY?

The Authenticity of the Bible

JESUS WRITES THROUGH Padgett that the text contained in the present Bible is *not* a true copy of what he said, or what was in the manuscripts of the original writers: "The sayings in the Epistles and in the Gospels and in Revelation to the effect that my blood saves from sin, are erroneous, and my disciples never wrote that false doctrine." It is a statement that Jesus emphatically repeats throughout his letters: "My blood has nothing to do with the redemption of mankind from sin, nor has my blood any effect in reconciling men to God or making them one with Him. The only thing that works this great result is the New Birth." (Padgett, 1958: II:149-150)

Jesus writes about the statements, attributed to his disciple John, that he is God and that his blood saves from sin: "John never wrote these statements as contained in his epistles and gospel, and he will write to you denying that he did. The Bible contains many truths and many of my sayings, but also, many statements that were never made by me or by the apostles, and my mission now is to correct all these errors." (Padgett, 1958: II:120)

John never said or wrote that by Jesus were all things created, and that Jesus, as God, came to earth and became human. "That is a mistake and an interpolation," says Jesus, "for I never was God, neither did I ever create any part of the universe. I was only a spirit of God sent by Him to work out man's salvation and show him the only way to the Heavenly Home that God has in keeping for those who receive the New Birth." (Padgett, 1958: II:35)

St. Luke, the writer of the third gospel and a follower of Jesus, writes about the authenticity of his gospel: "My gospel was not founded on anything I had personal knowledge of but upon the writings of others and the traditions which were the common knowledge of many Christians at that time." He said he knew several of the apostles and obtained much of his information from them. He also got information from members of the congregations to which these apostles preached. He writes:

> In my gospel, as now contained in the authorized version, there are many things that have been interpolated. This version was not based on what I wrote, but upon the pretended copies of my writings; and the persons who made these copies did not follow literally my writings, but added to my text and gave their own interpretations of what I had written in such a way as to destroy the true meaning of what was intended to be conveyed by my writings. (Padgett, 1958: II:166)

Luke says there are many truths contained in the gospel as now written in the Bible, and they are the truths of God, but there are also many errors which contradict these truths: "For instance, I never wrote that Jesus commanded his disciples to believe that the wine was his blood or the bread his body, and to eat and drink these things in remembrance of him." (Padgett, 1958: II:166)

In another message Luke writes, "Many truths that I did write are not contained therein—and so with the other gospels." (Padgett, 1958: I:78)

Jesus informs us that his spiritual guidance showing the way to the Celestial Kingdom was not well understood, not even by his intimate disciples. (John understood them the most.) Hence, they were not preserved in the Bible, as were his moral teachings. He states, "the original manuscripts were not written until many years after my death. Even in these manuscripts not many of my teachings as to the way that leads to this Celestial Kingdom, were contained; and afterwards when these manuscripts were copied, and the copies recopied, these important truths were not preserved—scarcely any." (Padgett, 1958: I:18)

However, Jesus says the fundamental ones, namely, that God is Love, and except a man be born again, he cannot enter into the Kingdom of Heaven, were retained. However, he writes that as time went on, and the recopying continued, fewer and fewer of his precepts were preserved. These copyists came to know less and less of the higher truths, and focused instead on Jesus' moral teachings. But that's not all.

> And in addition to this, these leaders changed even these moral truths and the interpretations of the early writers in such a way as to enable these leaders to attain to wealth and power and control over the common people in their beliefs and observances of worship. The God of Love then, to a large extent, became a God of hatred and wrath, inflicting punishment upon those who dared to disobey those injunctions that the hierarchy of

the church placed upon them as the demands and will of God. (Padgett, 1958: I:18-19)

Luke provides even more details about what happened to corrupt the gospels in a message in the Appendix entitled *Authenticity of the Bible.*

What About the Book of Revelation?

The Book of Revelation was composed as resistance literature to meet a crisis. Jesus tells us "the Revelation of John is not true—it is a mere allegory and not just as he wrote it, for it contains many things that are absurd and not in accord with the truths as I shall write them to you." John also wrote about the Book of Revelation, stating that he did not write much of it. Especially the part declaring the salvation of mankind through the blood of Jesus:

> Much of the matter contained in the Revelation I never wrote; but men or scribes who professed to copy the description of my vision, added to it for the purpose of incorporating therein the views of the Christians of that early day, so that their views might be emphasized and in union with similar views that had been added to the Gospels and Epistles in the copies which these same persons or their predecessors in these views had made. (Padgett, 1958: II:150)

John has been annoyed by this book of the Bible and its interpretations, as it does not contain his writings to any great extent. His ideas are not expressed or followed in the book. Jesus says John's Book of Revelation was merely a "revelation of a vision which he thought he saw while in a trance, as you mortals say. I mean that the real Revelation that he wrote is only the vision of a trance. So let not these things disturb you." (Padgett, 1958: II:150)

In John's own words: "My writings have been added to and all kinds of grotesque imagery interpolated so that the whole design and purpose of my writings were changed and destroyed." He says the book has no value, and is doing much harm to the cause of the truth as taught by Jesus, and should not be believed in for any purpose: "It has led many good men and honest and earnest seekers after the truth astray, and caused them to believe and teach false doctrines that have resulted in much darkness and stagnation in the development of human souls in their longings for the truth." He emphatically states that we should "discard its teachings, and any and all lessons that the preachers or others, who think that they can understand its meaning, attempt to teach." (Padgett, 1958: I:197)

What Does Jesus Say About His Second Coming?

"I am here to tell you that you had a cloud of witnesses as to your being selected to do my work," wrote Jesus, "and you have wondered why so many of my disciples and apostles and those called saints should come to you in such close succession, and all testify as to that one fact. Well, I caused them to come as I wished to establish your faith as to my being the true Jesus of the Bible, and as to your mission in regard to my work." (Padgett, 1958: III:161)

Another message from Jesus states his mission again: "Let me come to you often for you are the instrument that I wish to use in "MY NEW OR REPEATED GOSPEL OF GLAD TIDINGS TO THE HUMAN RACE." Jesus pleads with Padgett to be true to the trust being placed in him, and not to let the cares of the world keep him from spreading his gospel. "Come to the love of God in a more enlarged and truthful meaning and you will be my true follower. Let me lead you to the fountainhead of all the truths of God I have in store for humanity." (Padgett, 1958: II:5)

Jesus writes that we need to be awakened to the foolishness of focusing on materialism, and talks about the clouds that need to be lifted from our souls:

> The world needs a new awakening, and the infidelity and unbelief of men who think themselves wise but who are foolish as they will ultimately find out, and the material things, must not fill their souls much longer or they will suffer more than they can imagine. The material needs of mankind are not the only clouds that must be lifted from their souls. (Padgett, 1958: II:5)

The following quote from Jesus gives his views about apocalypticism:

> I know that it is believed and taught and emphasized, and men place all their hopes and expectations of a heaven of bliss on the statement, that I will at some time come in the clouds of heaven with a great shout, to earth, and by the power which they believe exists in me, establish the kingdom of God—a kind of kingdom in which I will be the king and rule supreme, and receive as my subjects those who believe in and worship me, and send those who do not into eternal damnation and outer darkness. Well, this is pitiable, untrue and all erroneous. (Padgett, 1958: I:15)

Jesus writes that the kingdom of God will never be established in this way because only man, himself, can bring about this kingdom. It was man who brought sin into the world, and only man can destroy sin.

Regarding the prophecy from Matthew 24 about the end of the world, Jesus writes that it referred to the fall of Jerusalem: "At that time—I mean just prior to and at the time of the destruction of Jerusalem—the whole world was in that condition that the prophecy speaks of—I did not know anything about the present condition of the earth, and could not have referred to these times, or to what may now happen among men." (Padgett, 1958: II:258)

The prophecy referred to the ending of the Jewish dispensation, and not to the end of the physical world. "[The world] was not to be destroyed at the time the prophecy was to be fulfilled," wrote Jesus, "and no man or Spirit now knows when the earth will cease to exist. Only God knows that, and he has never revealed it." (Padgett, 1958: II:258)

Jesus says we really don't need to be bothered by these things because he knows that such an event will never take place until God has worked out His plan for the ending of the world. Jesus wrote, "I believe it will be many centuries yet before such an ending to the earth and the visible world will take place. And I do not know that it ever will have an ending, and no human can foretell the same." (Padgett, 1958: II:258)

John, the disciple of Jesus, also writes fluently on the subject: "There is scarcely a greater error in the beliefs of men that retard the development of their souls than the belief that at some time Jesus will come in all his glory and power, and take men into his heaven, just as they are, in body, soul and spirit." (Padgett, 1958: I:338)

This belief has for a long time prevented many from seeking to develop their soul qualities, says John, "either as to the natural love or as to the Divine Love, for as a basis of their faith is that saying in the Bible that 'whosoever believes in the Lord Jesus Christ shall be saved'; and many thinking that they have this belief, are contented therein." They also believe that because of that belief, "they will be carried into

The spirits who know the truth have been working for centuries by means of spirit impression and revelation to help us learn the errors of our beliefs. John writes, "as our efforts have not been very successful, we concluded to use the means that we are now using, and to reveal to mankind in our own words and thoughts the truth of God as regards man and all things connected with him." (Padgett, 1958: I:338-339) For further enlightenment on this topic, the Appendix contains a message from Jesus entitled *Jesus Will Never Come as Prince Michael to Establish his Kingdom*.

Elizabeth, cousin of Mary, the mother of Jesus, also writes about his second coming: "So many spirits are engaged in this great work, which is the real second coming of Jesus—and which means the second coming of the ... privilege of receiving the Love." (Padgett, 1958: II:265)

Jesus writes in an early message to Padgett:

MY COMING TO YOU IS REALLY MY SECOND COMING ON EARTH, AND THE RESULT OF MY COMING IN THIS WAY WILL SATISFY AND FULFILL ALL THE PROMISES OF THE SCRIPTURES AS TO MY SECOND COMING. So let your belief in this important fact and your faith in me increase until you will have in your souls and minds no doubt as to WHAT MY PRESENT MISSION IS and as to what your work will be in making known to men my real purpose in revealing to them the great truths of the Father. (Padgett, 1958: I: 38-9)

—⋙⋘—

A Second New Testament?

The Padgett messages can be viewed as a supplement to the New Testament, a *Second New Testament*. In the same way that the New Testament was added to the Hebrew scriptures, it makes sense that Jesus' writings representing his second coming would be added onto the expression of his first coming. The New Testament writings all come from early Christian times and should be viewed from that context. The Padgett messages are twentieth century writings that deal with the same subject of Jesus Christ and his life, teachings, death, and resurrection.

In addition, they shed light on many details not in the New Testament. They are a spirit-filled, faith-building revelation by Jesus and his disciples—an important *direct* source for us to understand Jesus' teachings. In these humble messages, Jesus gives us the key to immortality and being at-one with God. The *salvation history* context of the New Testament is still important and valid, but the Padgett messages amplify, augment, and refine that salvation history, as this message from Jesus illustrates:

> ... in the Bible, which most of those professing to be Christians believe contains my sayings and teachings, is set forth this way to the Celestial Kingdom. The words are few and the way is plain, and no mystery prevents men from comprehending the meaning thereof. When I said, *"Except a man be born again, he cannot enter into the Kingdom of God,"* I disclosed the only and true way to this kingdom... The only way then is simply this: that men shall believe with all the sincerity of their minds and souls that this great Love of the Father is waiting to be

bestowed upon each and all of them, and that when they come to the Father in faith and earnest aspirations, this Love will not be withholden from them. (Padgett, 1958: I:23-24)

We all long for the truth. Our intellects are not satisfied with the present teachings of theology and many of the contradictions in the Bible. Jesus delivered a message through Padgett in which he advocated eliminating a "large part of the New and nearly the whole of the Old Testament" from Christian teachings. He further suggested the formulation of a faith based entirely on his sayings and some Bible writings. "Such a plan," writes Jesus, "is one that should be investigated by the thinking Christians of the present day, and in a modified way adopted." (Padgett, 1958: I:212)

CHAPTER 10

THE DIVINE DARE FROM JESUS

JESUS AND HIS Celestial colleagues challenged Padgett and his friends to try an experiment—to pray for God's Love. This resulted in Padgett's soul becoming transformed and in harmony with Jesus so he could deliver important messages to humanity. His friends also felt the transforming effects. Since that time, many others have tried this Divine Dare, with tremendous success.

The challenge is simply this: Two times a day (at least), for the next thirty (30) days, say the prayer from Jesus. Even better, memorize it. This prayer is called the Prayer Perfect because Jesus wrote that it's the *only* prayer needed. (You can find it at the end of the Appendix.)

Once you know the content of the prayer, saying it word-for-word is not necessary. The words are not important. You don't even need words. It is the intensity of longing, your crying out to God through your soul, that is most crucial. And what it is you are longing for. God hears the yearnings of our souls, not our words. The words are just a soul-prompt, if needed.

This does not have to be a challenge to your current religious beliefs. Your beliefs do not matter. What is most important is to speak directly to God, soul to Soul, *asking for His Love, and sending your love to God.* The benefits are many, as my friends and I testify. Happiness. Inner peace. Love overflowing. Divine Love is a real substance, God's very essence, and our souls become altered upon receiving it.

I have heard dozens of testimonies. My friend, author Joan Warden, compiled and edited two collections of true stories of soul awakenings and spiritual experiences from Divine Love seekers. You can access her books at www.divineloveforthesoul.com. Below are excerpts from the reports of results obtained by some of our friends. And Joan gives her own testimony about how God's Love affects her.

> "Besides delight and happiness, which always comes to me when our Heavenly Father sends His Divine Love," wrote Joan, "I experience different degrees of warmth in my heart. And it always depends on the circumstance, whether the Love will remain the same temperature or increase to become hot, hot, and hotter. And, of course, it also depends on how open my soul is to receiving it, whether it just lasts a minute or goes on for days."

Joan loves being in "the Divine Love spiritual zone" because her "soul never closes and Divine Love continually pours in. This is when I'm receiving my spiritual food and my physical appetite goes away. It's a great way to get and stay in shape without having to exercise (thank you, Father!). And this is just one of the many benefits I enjoy when receiving His wondrous Love." (Warden, 2015: 265-266) Joan has been devoted to Jesus' Divine Love messages for over thirty-seven years. She is a trustee of the Foundation.

My Divine Love sister, Holly Bianco, a registered nurse and trustee of the Foundation Church of Divine Truth, testifies about her first meeting with the angels and feeling God's Presence, after earnest prayer from her soul for God's Love to flow in. This, she said, caused her spiritual faculties to awaken. "At first, I started to perceive someone watching me. Then soon after, I was able to come into contact with my mother, Helen, who had died of cancer six years prior. Her voice was clear and she had the same personality and expression as she did on earth but most of all she was so happy to be able to connect with me."

Holly did not only hear her mother's voice, but many other angelic spirits came to greet her. "I could hear beautiful voices, both male and female angels, and they sounded as if they were 10 feet tall, beautiful and majestic in nature but at the same time soft and gentle. They wanted me to know that life continues, that God's Love is real, and the messages received through James E. Padgett were truly given to him from the spirits who wrote through him." (Warden, 2015: 126-127) Holly has been a follower of Jesus' Divine Love teachings for over thirty-seven years. She says, "no other spiritual source, including the Bible, has ever brought [me] closer to God or even opened the door to the reality of spiritual things than the Divine Love."

The Great Challenge produced results for my comrade, Michael Nedbal, an author with over a dozen published works. He wrote:

> The messages spoke of this great experiment. If you would pray to God for His Divine Love, you would eventually feel a burning sensation in your soul. I tried the experiment. I prayed three times a day for two weeks. At first, I felt nothing. But as I let go of my mind's judgments and expectations, I started to feel a sense of peace. And then towards the end of the second week it happened—I felt the area around my solar plexus begin to warm and burn. It was a wonderful feeling.

I finally received tangible proof of God's existence. He was hearing my prayers and He answered.... For the first time in my life, I knew I had a soul and that I had a direct connection with God! (Warden, 2012: 53)

Michael continued to pray and read the Padgett messages, with the faith that as his prayers continued, his soul would take on more and more of God's Divine Love and gradually become transformed. "As water may become colored by an ingredient foreign to itself, which changes not only its appearance but its qualities," he wrote, "so the Divine Love changes the appearance and qualities of the soul. And with this transformation comes soul perceptions—you start to sense your connection with God and the presence of the Celestial Angels, who assist and guide you in your life here on earth." (Warden, 2012: 53-54)

Michael further reported that "the presence of God's Divine Love in my soul has changed my very existence. I call it 'Being in the Love.' There is no anger, hatred, jealousy, fear, or feelings of unworthiness when God's Divine Love burns in my soul. There is only peace, harmony, understanding, Love, and a strong connection with God." (Warden, 2012: 54) Michael became ordained as a Divine Love minister in 1998. He is a trustee and vice president of the Foundation Church of Divine Truth.

Carolyn Stokes, a Divine Love friend for over thirty years, describes her first experience of receiving God's Love while in a meditative state: "The next thing I was aware of could only be described as rapture. I felt brilliant warmth of golden-white light invade me. I felt peace, fulfillment, joyousness and love. It was overwhelming, yet I felt no fear. I felt like I was being drawn high up in the sky. I was in bliss. I wanted for nothing. I felt complete. The connection I felt was to God." (Warden, 2012: 58-59) Carolyn has been a follower of the

Divine Love Messages for over forty years and was ordained in 1993. She is a holistic health educator, licensed masseuse, and president of Divine Love Ministry, Inc.

David Lampron, a Divine Love ordained minister since 1977 and president of the Foundation Church of Divine Truth since 1996, reported on his first experience receiving God's Love:

> There was no way that I could preconceive what a direct response from God would be like. All I can tell you is that I wanted God. With all the longing of my soul, that had been slowly but surely cultivated for Him within me over the years, I began to pray as I never prayed before. With the open heart of a child, and with a great desire borne of years of former searching, I prayed to our Great Father with all the energy and soul longing I could muster from the depths of my being. My words were clothed in terms of simply wanting to feel His Presence, to know Him in some direct, personal, and intimate way.... And although my prayer did not ask for an immediate response ... an immediate response did come nevertheless, much to my surprise and wonderment.
>
> What words can I select to express such sublimity? How does one describe an "orgasm of soul"? How does one describe a momentary feeling and absolute knowledge of immortality? How does one describe the uniting of Soul with soul where Personality and personality, for a moment of time, merge as one? How does one describe a Living Substance Divine that permeates and fills the soul with ineffable bliss? (Warden, 2012: 61-62)

My friend Ruth Duvall, an award-winning poet and author, described her experience of receiving Divine Love: "I felt the warmth of loving arms around me and through me and the only way I can describe the following experience was—it was like a nuclear explosion in my soul. It was a total white out of Love. It was so powerful and penetrating ... Mere words do not do it justice." (Warden, 2012: 94) Ruth started The Hope Prayer Box ministry which has spread around the world. She has been part of the Divine Love community for eighteen years.

This is a small sampling of the testimonies available about the transforming power of God's Essence. Give it a try. You have nothing to lose and everything to gain. Everyone can do this and get results. Once you have tasted the sweetness of God's Love, you will not want to stop receiving it, ever!

Everyone feels this connection with God differently. I would love to know what happens for you. If you feel moved to share your experience, please write to me at secondnewtestament@gmail.com.

> **"His listening ear is always open to the earnest aspirations of His children who come to Him with the true longings of the soul. You have the secret of reaching the Father's Love, and on all occasions, when you feel that you need that Love or desire a nearness to the Father, use the secret and you will not be disappointed."**
>
> **—Jesus (Padgett, 1958: I:59-60)**

CONCLUSION

"The day the power of love overrules the love of power, the world will know peace."

—Mahatma Gandhi

"God has no religion."

—Mahatma Gandhi

WE WILL EVENTUALLY have harmony and peace on earth. Evil will be eradicated. It's a matter of time, and the timing depends on us. "That all men will ultimately be brought into harmony with God, in either the natural love or in the higher one, is certain, and that all sin and error will finally be eradicated from God's universe is decreed, but the time will depend to a great extent, upon the wills and desires of men." (Padgett, 1958: I:121)

Jesus' great mission and teaching in coming to earth was to show the way to the Celestial Kingdom. A secondary aspect of his mission was to teach a way to redemption from sin, resulting in the purification of the natural love. "And to my great regret and to the untold injury to man," writes Jesus, "my moral teachings were more at large set forth in portions of the Bible, as now accepted, than were my teachings of the higher truths."

The more Divine Love is present in the soul, the less tendency that soul has toward evil, and takes on more qualities of the divine nature. "The possession of this Divine Love," writes Jesus, "also means the absence of those desires and longings of what is called the natural man, which produce selfishness and unkindness and other qualities which create sin and error, and prevent the existence of this true brotherhood which men so earnestly desire as the forerunner of peace and goodwill." (Padgett, 1958: I:133)

"The Father is all goodness and love and truth, and forgiveness, and kindness," continues Jesus, "and these qualities the souls of men become possessed of, when they receive and possess the Divine Love." These qualities, once possessed, never leave or change. A kinship of humanity founded on these qualities will be built on a rock. It will continue to live and grow. It will become purer and firmer in its binding effect. Great results will flow from it, because its foundation is in the divine nature of God, which does not change or vary and is never disappointing.

A kinship created in this way is "the only true brotherhood that will make for man a kind of heaven on earth, and banish wars and hatred and strife and selfishness... all mankind will be truly brothers, without reference to race or sect or intellectual acquirements." (Padgett, 1958: I:133-134)

"There will be a religion of the future and a comprehensive and final one," Jesus states in another letter, "and it will be founded upon the truth which you are now receiving, for it will be inclusive of all the other religions, so far as the truths that they contain are concerned, with the addition of the greatest of all truths affecting mortals—the new birth and transforming of the human soul into the divine." Jesus writes that when a comparative analysis of existing religions is made with his teachings through the Padgett messages "there will be very little conflict in the vital principles, and my teachings will only add to the old teachings that which all men can accept." (Padgett, 1958: I:300)

We can become fully transformed by God's Love while a mortal, like Jesus accomplished. It depends only upon ourselves how rapid our progress is into the divine. "You need not wait until you come to the spirit world in order to make a rapid progression," writes Jesus, "although it will be more difficult for you to progress while in the flesh." Nonetheless, he says, "wonderful progress may be made while in the flesh, and you have been told the secret of this progress." (Padgett, 1958: I:5)

It is more difficult to progress on earth. Many circumstances, surroundings, and limitations prevent our soul aspirations and faith from working freely—conditions that do not exist after becoming an inhabitant of the spirit world. "Nevertheless," writes Jesus, "the soul of man may receive this Divine Love without limitations and to an abundance that will make him a new creature." (Padgett, 1958: I:133) This is our highest potential!

The biggest secret of the Universe is in the simple words "God is Love." And that His great Love can be within us. If we all knew about and realized our divinity, our kinship with God, our most difficult struggles and hardships would be over.

The veils are being lifted at an accelerating rate. Many honest, kind, noble and helpful people are focusing on enlightenment— individuals of great goodwill, undying faith, and love—dedicated to learning and teaching spiritual skills. We are in the midst of an evolution of consciousness, a new reformation in not just Christian thinking, but religious thinking altogether. We are at the dawning of a shining new reality—a world of kindness and harmony, where we are all bound together in Love. We will serve each other with compassion. Sickness will be eradicated. The sorrows of this day and time will be a distant memory.

We are now one hundred years into the second coming, and the transformation is upon us. More people in the world are receiving Divine Love than ever before, including many who are close to the full transformation of soul written about and demonstrated by Jesus. And more are joining the path of Divine Love every day. One of the beauties of this manifestation of the second coming is that it did not just happen as a physical event on our terrestrial earth. It keeps happening spiritually as people are drawn to it. A personal, private experience of the second coming. It's happening right now. At this very moment, Jesus is touching someone's soul with the good news.

As Buddhism is a fresh revelation of the same basic teachings which originally inspired Hinduism (like a "second coming" within Hinduism) ... so, too, the Padgett messages encapsulate a fresh revelation of the same basic teachings which originally inspired Christianity—illumination about connecting with God in Love.

Love is always the answer, especially God's Love. My most fervent and constant prayer is that all humanity will awaken to the pure experience and knowledge of God's Divine Essence, and the purpose of the Holy Spirit to fill their souls with that Essence. The Bible promises this in John 14:18: "I will not leave you orphaned: I am coming to you." And John 14:26: "But the Advocate, the Holy Ghost, whom the Father will send ... will teach you everything, and remind you of all that I have said to you." This is the true destiny of humanity. It is in our power, and we are powerful beings. We only have to choose.

The world cries out for healing, and, especially, for knowledge about God. We must bring this vital message of Divine Love to the world. Love is the currency on the other side. We must *be* the Love.

———— ✢ ————

"My second coming will be as the still small voice that speaks to every man and tells him that love is the only thing that is necessary for him to have, and when he gets that in his soul, all the sins and hatred and desires for evil will pass away."

—Jesus, IV:174

———— ✢ ————

BIBLIOGRAPHY

Alexander, Eben with Ptolemy Tompkins, *The Map of Heaven: How Science, Religion, and Ordinary People Are Proving the Afterlife*, New York: Simon & Schuster, Inc., 2014.

Alexander, Eben, *Proof of Heaven: A Neurosurgeon's Journey into the Afterlife*, New York: Simon & Schuster, Inc., 2012.

Anthony, Mark, *Evidence of Eternity: Communicating with Spirits for Proof of the Afterlife*, Woodbury: Llewellyn Publications, 2015.

Boadt, Lawrence, *Reading the Old Testament: An Introduction*, New York: Paulist Press, 1984.

Botkin, Allan L. and Craig Hogan, *Induced After Death Communication: A Miraculous Therapy for Grief and Loss*, Charlottesville: Hampton Roads Publishing Company, Inc., 2014.

Bragdon, Emma, *A Source Book for Helping People with Spiritual Problems*, Woodstock: Lightening Up Press, 1994.

Braude, Ann, *Radical Spirits: Spiritualism and Women's Rights in Nineteenth-Century America*, Boston: Beacon Press, 1989.

Bruce, Frederick F., *Are the New Testament Documents Reliable*, Grand Rapids: Wm. B. Eerdmans Publishing Co., 1954.

Brunner, Emil, *The Divine-Human Encounter*, Philadelphia: The Westminster Press, 1943.

Buck, Harry, *People of the Lord*, New York: The Macmillan Company, 1966.

Carlston, Charles E., "The canon—problems and benefits", *Andover Newton Review* 2(No.1):33-43 (1991).

Champlain, Sandra, *We Don't Die: A Skeptic's Discovery of Life After Death*, New York: Imbue Press, 2013.

Couliano, Ioan P., *The Tree of Gnosis*, San Francisco: Harper Collins Publishers, 1992.

Craig, Clarence T., *The Beginning of Christianity*, New York: Abingdon-Cokesbury Press, 1943.

Diamandis, Peter H and Steven Kotler, *Abundance: The Future Is Better Than You Think*, New York: Free Press, 2012.

Dodd, C. H., *The Authority of the Bible*, New York: Harper & Brothers, 1929.

Doyle, Arthur C., *The New Revelation*, New York: George H. DoranCo., 1918.

Duling, Dennis C. and Norman Perrin, *The New Testament: Proclamation and Parenesis, Myth and History*, 3rd edition, Fort Worth: Harcourt Brace College Publishers, 1994.

Eadie, Betty J., *Embraced by the Light*, Placerville: Gold Leaf Press, 1992.

Gottwald, Norman, *The Tribes of Yahweh*, Maryknoll, N.Y.: Orbis Books, 1979.

Grof, Stanislav and Christina Grof, *Spiritual Emergency: When Transformation Becomes a Crisis*, New York: Jeremy P. Tarcher, 1989.

Grof, Christina and Stanislav Grof, *The Stormy Search for the Self: A Guide to Personal Growth through Transformational Crisis*, New York: Jeremy P. Tarcher, 1990.

Groothuis, Douglas R., "The New Testament canon faces the New Age challenge", *Epiphany* ll:17-20 (1991).

Haddow, Angus, "Out-of-Body and Near-Death Experiences: Their Impact on Religious Beliefs," *Journal of Religion & Psychical Research* 14(No.2): 75-85 (1991).

Harrington, John B., *Issues in Christian Thought*, New York: McGraw-Hill, Inc., 1968.

Heine, Ronald E., "Montanus, Montanism", *The Anchor Bible Dictionary* 4:898-902 (1992).

Hennecke, E. and W. Schneemelcher, *New Testament Apocrypha*, trans. R. McL. Wilson, vol. 1, Philadelphia: Westminster Press, 1963.

Higgins, Joseph and R. Craig Hogan (editors), *Afterlife Resources: 2017 Symposium Attendees and Presenters*, Normal: Afterlife Research and Education Institute, Inc., 2017.

Hill, Roy L., *Jesus and the Near-Death Experience: Testimonies of the Ascended Christ*, Hove: White Crow Books, 2017.

Hogan, R. Craig (editor), *New Developments in Afterlife Communication: Proceedings of the 38th Annual Conference of the Academy for Spiritual and Consciousness Studies*, Loxahatchee: Academy for Spiritual and Consciousness Studies, 2014.

Hogan, R. Craig, *Your Eternal Self*, Greater Reality Publications, 2009.

Holy Bible: New Revised Standard Version with Apocrypha, Ed. B. M. Metzger, New York: Oxford University Press, 1989.

Hoover, Roy W., "How the Books of the New Testament Were Chosen", *Bible Review* 9:44-47 (1993).

Jewett, Robert, *Jesus Against the Rapture: Seven Unexpected Prophecies*, Philadelphia: The Westminster Press, 1979.

Kee, Howard C., *Understanding the New Testament*, 4th edition, Englewood Cliffs: Prentice-Hall, 1983.

Kelsey, *Discernment: A Study in Ecstasy and Evil*, New York: Paulist Press, 1978.

Klimo, Jon, *Channeling*, Los Angeles: Jeremy P. Tarcher, Inc., 1987.

Koch, Klaus, *The Prophets*, Philadelphia: Fortress Press, 1983.

Koester, Helmut, *Introduction to the New Testament, Volume 2: History and Literature of Early Christianity*, New York: Walter De Gruyter, 1982.

Kübler-Ross, Elisabeth, *On Death and Dying*, New York: Macmillan, 1969.

Lane, David, "The Spiritual Crucible: A Critical Guide to America's Religious/Cultic Renaissance," *The Cultic Studies Journal* 3(No.1): 78-92 (1986).

Lindblom, Johannes, *Prophecy in Ancient Israel*, Philadelphia: Fortress Press, 1962.

Linebarger, John M., "History meets theology: three recent books about the canon: a review article", *Crux* 27:34-37 (1991).

Metzger, Bruce M., *The Canon of the New Testament: Its Origin, Development, and Significance*, Oxford: Clarendon Press, 1989.

Metzger, Bruce M. (translation committee head), *Holy Bible: New Revised Standard Version with Apocrypha*, New York: Oxford University Press, 1989.

Metzger, Bruce M., *The Text of the New Testament: Its Transmission, Corruption, and Restoration*, New York: Oxford University Press, 1968.

Moody, Raymond, Jr., *Life After Life*, Covington: Mockingbird Books, 1975.

Moody, Raymond, Jr., *Reflections on Life After Life*, Covington: Mockingbird Books, 1977.

Morse, Melvin with Paul Perry, *Parting Visions: Uses and Meanings of Pre-Death, Psychic, and Spiritual Experiences*, New York: Villard Books, 1994.

Oldenburg, Don, "The Spiritual Crisis Mode," *Washington Post* article, November 12, 1994.

Padgett, James E., *True Gospel Revealed Anew by Jesus*, Vol. I, II, III, IV, Washington D.C.: Foundation Church of the New Birth, 1958.

Quebedeaux, Richard, *By What Authority*, San Francisco: Harper & Row, 1982.

Redfield, James, *Celestine Prophecy*, New York: Warner Books, Inc., 1993.

Schwartz, Gary, *The Sacred Promise: How Science Is Discovering Spirit's Collaboration with Us in Our Daily Lives*, New York: Atria Books, 2011.

Sellin, E. and G. Fohrer, (translation by D. Green), *Introduction to the Old Testament*, Nashville: Abingdon Press, 1968.

Smith, Huston, *Forgotten Truth: The Primordial Tradition*, New York: Harper & Row, 1976.

Steiger, Brad, *Revelation, The Divine Fire: An Investigation of Men and Women Who Claim to be in Spiritual Communication with a Higher Intelligence*, Englewood Cliffs: Prentice-Hall, Inc., 1973.

Tabori, Paul, *Companions of the Unseen*, New York: University Books, 1968.

Trismegistus, Hermes, *A Holy Book of Hermes Trismegistus Addressed to Asclepius*, Whitefish: Kessinger Publishing, 2010.

Trismegistus, Hermes, *A Secret Discourse of Hermes Trismegistus Concerning Rebirth*, Whitefish: Kessinger Publishing, 2010.

Twiss, Sumner B. and Walter H. Conser, Jr. (editors), *Experience of the Sacred: Readings in the Phenomenology of Religion*, Hanover: Brown University Press, 1992.

Von Rad, Gerhard, *The Message of the Prophets*, New York: Harper & Row, 1967.

Warden, Joan (editor), *Divine Love for the Soul: God's Gift of Love*, 2012.

Warden, Joan (editor), *God's Divine Love is the Solution: A Collection of True Stories of Soul Awakenings, Spiritual Experiences, Inspirational Essays, Poetry and Messages from Divine Angels*, 2015.

Weber, Timothy P., *Living in the Shadow of the Second Coming: American Premillennialism, 1875-1982*, Chicago: The University of Chicago Press, 1987.

White, John Wesley, *Re-Entry*, Minneapolis: World Wide Publications, 1975.

Whitehead, Alfred North, *Science and the Modern World*, New York: The Macmillan Co., 1925

Wilson, Robert R., *Prophecy and Society in Ancient Israel*, Philadelphia: Fortress Press, 1980.

Wilson, Susanne J., *Soul Smart: What the Dead Teach Us About Spirit Communication*, Madison: Christine F. Anderson Publishing, 2017.

Zammit, Victor and Wendy Zammit, *A Lawyer Presents the Evidence for the Afterlife*, Guildford: White Crow Books, 2013.

http://www.afterliferesearch.org/arei-initiatives-instrumental-trans communication/

History Channel (August 31, 2019), *The UnXplained: Mysterious Phenomena*

APPENDIX

13 Messages Received Through James Padgett

Table of Contents

First Four Messages from Jesus:
- *Jesus Wants the World to Follow His Teachings*
- *Jesus is the Way, the Truth and the Life; Not God, but Sent by God*
- *First Formal Message by Jesus–Who He Really Was; Misconceptions in the New Testament*
- *Divine Love Reaching Out to Every Man; Padgett is the Instrument to Receive the Truths*

Jesus' Mission in Writing These Messages is His Second Coming on Earth (by Jesus)

Jesus Will Never Come as Prince Michael to Establish His Kingdom (by Jesus)

Destiny of Man Without Divine Love Who Dies Only with Natural Love and Belief in the Creeds and Dogmas of the Churches (by Jesus)

Birth and Life of Jesus Up to His Public Ministry (by Jesus)

Authenticity of the Bible (by Luke)

Importance of the Jews Learning Jesus' Correct Teachings (by Moses)

Woman of Endor Was Not a Wicked Woman as Many Believe (by Saul of the Old Testament)

Genesis Copied from Ancient Writings on Creation and Fall of Man (by Leytergus, ancient spirit)

The Only Prayer Needed (by Jesus)

APPENDIX

Jesus Wants the World to Follow His Teachings – September 12, 1914 (II:1)

I Am Here, *Jesus.*

God is love and they that worship Him in spirit and love will not be forsaken.

I came to tell you that you are very near the kingdom, only believe and pray to the Father and you will soon know the truth, and the truth will make you free. *You were hard hearted and sinful, but now that you are seeking the light I will come to you and help you, only believe and you will soon see the truth of my teachings. Go not in the way of the wicked for their end is punishment and long suffering. Let your love for God and your fellow man increase.

You are not in condition for further writing. I will come to you again when you are stronger. Yes, it is Jesus and I want the world to follow the teachings of my words.

Goodbye and may the Holy Spirit bless you as I do.

Jesus Christ.

*Mr. Padgett had a vision of Jesus many years before he knew he had the gift of automatic writing. During the vision, Jesus looked at him with a great love and sympathy as if he wanted him to become a true follower of him.

———→✠←———

Jesus is the Way, the Truth and the Life; Not God, but Sent by God – September 24, 1914 (II:2)

I Am Here, Jesus.

Be of good cheer for I am with you always. Do not let your heart fear, for the Lord is your keeper and He will be your guide and shield. Only believe and trust in Him and you will soon be born again into the spiritual world of His kingdom. Let me teach you and give you the thoughts that He gave me while on earth. Let me show you that the things of this world are not the things that save the soul from sin and unhappiness. Be a true follower of your God.

It [the New Birth] is the flowing of the Holy Spirit into the soul of a man and the disappearing of all that tended to keep it in a condition of sin and error. It is not the workings of the man's own will but the grace of God. It is the love of God that passes all understanding. You will soon experience the change and then you will be a happy man and fit to lead others to the truths of God. Let your heart be open to the knockings of the Spirit and keep your mind free from thoughts of sin. Be a man who loves his God and his fellow man. Your love is only now of the earthly kind, but it will soon be of the things spiritual.

You must not let the cares of this world keep you from God. Let His Spirit come into your soul. Your will is the thing that determines whether you will become a child of God or not. Unless you are willing to let the Holy Spirit enter into your heart it will not do so. Only the voluntary submission to or acceptance of the Holy Spirit will make the change.

I was the instrument in God's hands of leading men to His favor and love. When I said I am the Way, the Truth and the Life, I meant that through my teachings and example men should be able to find God. I was not God and never claimed to be. The worship of me as a God is blasphemous and I did not teach it. I am a son of God as you are. Do not let the teachings of men lead you to worship me as a God. I am not. The trinity is a mistake of the writers of the Bible. There is no trinity—only one God, the Father. He is one and alone. I am His teacher of truth—the Holy Spirit is His messenger and dispenser of love to mankind. We are only His instruments in bringing man to a union with Him. **I am not the equal of my Father—He is the only true God.** I came from the spirit world to earth and took the form of man, but I did not become a God—only the son of my Father. You also lived as a spirit in that kingdom, but you took the form of man merely as a son of your Father. You are the same as I am, except as to spiritual development, and you may become as greatly developed as myself. **I am the only son when on earth who until then had become vested with the Divine Love of God to the extent of being wholly free from sin and error when I lived in the flesh.** My life was not a life of earthly pleasure or sin, but was given wholly to my Father's work. I was His only son in that light. He was my Father as I knew Him to be. He is not a spirit of form like myself or yourself.

I was born as you were born. I was the son of Mary and Joseph and not born of the Holy Spirit as it is written in the Bible. I was only a human being as regards my birth and physical existence. The account in the New Testament is not true and was written by those who knew not what they wrote. They have done the cause of God's truths much injury. Let not your belief in that error keep you from seeing that my teachings are the truth. Be only a believer of God and His truths and you will soon be in the kingdom. You will soon be able to understand as I understand.

Good night.

Jesus Christ.

———➤✠◄———

First Formal Message by Jesus–Who He Really Was; Misconceptions in the New Testament – September 28, 1914 (I:366-367)

I Am Here, *Jesus.*

You are my true brother and will soon have the Love of our Father in your heart. Do not be discouraged or cast down for the Holy Spirit will soon fill your heart with the Love of the Father, and then you will be most happy and full of light and power to help yourself and fellowmen.

Go to your Father for His help. Go in prayer, firmly believing and you soon will feel His Love in your heart. My teachings, I know, you will receive in the course of time, and you will then see that your understanding will be greatly enlarged so that you will know that I am the Father's son as I explained it to you a few nights ago. You can and will receive the Father's Love so that you will not need to go through the expiation in the spirit world.

I was not conceived by the Holy Spirit, as it is taught by the preachers and teachers who are now leading mankind in the doctrines of the churches. I was born as you were born, and my earthly father was Joseph. I was conceived by God's Spirit in the sense that I was born free from sin and error, while all other human beings were born in sin and error. I never was a human being so far as my spiritual existence is concerned, as I was always free from sin and error, but I had all the feelings and longings of a human being which were not of sin. My love was human as well as spiritual, and I was subject to all the feelings of sympathy and love that any other human being was. Do not understand that I was with desires and longings for the pleasures of the world which the human passions created. I was not, only I was capable of deep feeling, and could feel and know the suffering and distress of humanity.

Yes, I will, and you will learn that many errors were written by the writers of the Bible. I will show you that the many alleged sayings of mine were not said by me or did not express my teachings of the truth. Her teachings of Christian Science do not express the true meaning of truth and love as I taught them. She is in error as to the ideas that God is spirit only, a spirit of mind. He is a spirit of everything that belongs to His Being. He is not only Mind, but Heart, Soul and Love.

You are too weak to write more. You have my blessing and also that of the Holy Spirit.

Jesus the Christ.

———✤———

Divine Love Reaching Out to Every Man; Padgett is the Instrument to Receive the Truths – September 29, 1914 (II:4-5)

Christ Jesus is here and wishes to write to you about the love of God and the needs of mankind.

Let your mind be free from all thoughts of evil and sin. The love of God is reaching out for every man so that the meanest will be the object of His care. Do not let the thought that He is only loving the good and righteous lead you to think that you must seek the company of these favored ones only. Let the lost and unhappy be the objects of your efforts to show them the way to the Father.

You will have an opportunity in receiving our messages to teach all mankind the love of God for His children, and that they are the children of His greatest care and love. Be only earnest in your efforts to spread the truths which I shall teach you in my communications, and you will be a successful laborer in the work which the Father has decreed you to do. Give your best endeavors to the spreading of the messages and you will not only save the souls of the blinded and lost, but also will hasten the coming of the kingdom in your own life and heart. Let me come to you often for **you are the instrument that I wish to use in "MY NEW OR REPEATED GOSPEL OF GLAD TIDINGS TO THE HUMAN RACE."** Be true to the trust that I shall impose in you and let not the cares of the world keep you from spreading my gospel. Come to the love of God in a more enlarged and truthful meaning and you will be my true follower. Let me lead you to the fountainhead of all the truths of God I have in store for humanity.

My own love and power will guide you and keep you in the way of Light and Truth that you may teach to your fellow man. Your own soul must be first purified and then you will be able to show others the power and love that I have for them.

You are not to seek the help of other spirits until I teach you the truths of my Father. He is the only one who has the power to save men from their sins and errors. Be true and earnest in your work, and don't let other things distract your mind or work from the task set before you. The world needs a new awakening, and the infidelity and unbelief of men who think themselves wise but who are foolish as they will ultimately find out, and the material things must not fill their souls much longer or they will suffer more than they can imagine. The material needs of mankind are not the only clouds that must be lifted from their souls.

You are too weak to write more now. Yes, but I am not able to write more now because you are not in condition. You must stop writing now.

Jesus Christ.

———— ❉ ————

Jesus' Mission in Writing These Messages is His Second Coming on Earth
– December 2, 1915 (I:38-39)

I Am Here. *Jesus.*

I have heard your discussion tonight, and am pleased at the soul understanding of my truths which you and your friend [L.R. Stone was present] seem to have and I now feel that you are both progressing to that point where you will soon be in a condition to fully understand WHAT MY MISSION IS IN WRITING THESE MESSAGES. You have said truly that my new revelation of the truths of the soul is what mankind needs at this time, and what men will be in condition to accept as the real truths of God's love and of His laws. MY COMING TO YOU IS REALLY MY SECOND COMING ON EARTH, AND THE RESULT OF MY COMING IN THIS WAY WILL SATISFY AND FULFILL ALL THE PROMISES OF THE SCRIPTURES AS TO MY SECOND COMING.

So let your belief in this important fact and your faith in me increase until you will have in your souls and minds no doubt as to what my present mission is, and as to what your work will be in making known to men my real purpose in revealing to them the great truths of the Father.

I will not write more tonight, but say keep up your courage and believe, and the time will soon come when you will be able to receive my messages in all their fullness, and with such rapidity that the spreading of these truths will not be delayed. I am with you and will be a faithful friend and brother, sticking closer to you than any earthly brother. With all my love and blessings, I am your loving brother and friend,

Jesus.

———→✳←———

*Jesus Will Never Come as Prince Michael to Establish His Kingdom –
August 13, 1916 (I:336-338)*
I Am Here. *Jesus.*

I was with you tonight and heard the address of the preacher and
the explanation of the cause of the great war that is now raging in
Europe and it was a very intelligent and truthful one and the real
foundation of the war.

I will not come as the Prince Michael, as the preacher said, to establish
my Kingdom on earth and take into me those whose names are written
in the book and destroy those whose names are not therein written, for
I have already come and am now in the world working to turn men's
hearts to God and to teach them the way by which they may become
at-one with the Father and receive into their souls the Divine Love.

In no other way will I ever come to men on earth for they will
not need me as a visible king with the powers and armies of the spirit
world in visible form to subdue the evil that exists. There will arise no
Satan to fight against me or my followers in the sense that the preacher
teaches, for besides the fact that I am already in the world fighting for
the salvation of men, there is no Satan. The only devils or evil spirits
who are trying to influence men to evil thoughts and actions are the
spirits of men which still retain all their sins and wickedness, and the
evil that exists in the hearts of men themselves.

How pitiable it is that the preacher and his followers believe that
the spirits of men who have died the natural death, are also dead
and resting in the grave or in oblivion, waiting for the great day of
my appearance on earth, as they say, in order to come again into life
and be called by me into my Kingdom. How much they lose by such
beliefs, and how great and surprising will be their awakening when
they pass through the change called death.

THERE WILL BE NO BATTLE OF ARMAGEDDON, ONLY AS EACH MAN, OR THE SOUL OF EACH MAN, IS NOW FIGHTING THE BATTLE BETWEEN SIN AND RIGHTEOUSNESS. THIS IS THE ONLY BATTLE THAT WILL EVER BE FOUGHT BETWEEN THE PRINCE OF PEACE AND SATAN. EACH SOUL MUST FIGHT ITS OWN BATTLE, AND IN THAT FIGHT THE POWERS OF GOD, BY HIS INSTRUMENTS, WHICH NEVER CEASE TO WORK, WILL BE USED TO HELP THAT SOUL OVERCOME THE GREAT ENEMY, SIN, WHICH IS OF MAN'S CREATION.

These teachings of the preacher do great harm to mankind in that they cause the individual man to believe, that I, as the Prince of Peace, will come in mighty power, and in one fell swoop will destroy evil and all who personify it, and thereby do the work which each individual man must do.

I know that it will be very difficult to persuade the people of this sect that what they teach and what they conclude the Bible teaches is not true, but I hope that when my truths are brought to light and men have the opportunity to learn the truth, that many of them will halt in the security of their beliefs and attempt to understand these truths, as they must understand them, either in the mortal life or in the spirit world, in order to enter the Kingdom of God.

As to these prophecies of Daniel, they have no application to the present condition of the world, and so far as they were written by him or by any other prophet, they related only to the times in which they were written. No man, inspired or not, and no spirit, had the omniscience to foretell these wonderful things that are now taking place in the world, and any attempts to apply these supposed prophecies to the happenings of the present day are without justification and the results of the imaginations of men that the occurrences fit the prophecies.

PEACE WILL COME, BUT NOT AS THE RESULT OF ANY BATTLE OF ARMAGEDDON, OR ANY OTHER BATTLE BASED UPON THE PRINCIPLES WHICH THE PREACHER APPLIES TO THESE PROPHECIES. AS I HAVE SAID, THIS BATTLE IS GOING ON ALL THE TIME, AND IT IS AN INDIVIDUAL FIGHT BETWEEN THE SINFUL SOUL AND THE CREATURES OF MAN'S DISOBEDIENCE.

So do not waste your time in reading or listening to these unreal and foundationless teachings of men who think that they have discovered the intentions of God with reference to the destiny of nations.

I will not write more tonight, but at some time I may say more on this subject, though its only importance is that it attracts men's attention away from the truth and creates beliefs which do harm.

I will soon come and write another message of truth. I am with you, as I told you, trying to help you and to show you the way to that New Birth which is yours and all others who will follow my instructions. I love you as a younger brother and will continue to bless you with my influence and prayers. So doubt not and pray to the Father and you will find the truth in greater fullness and receive corresponding happiness. I will now stop. Your brother and friend,

Jesus.

————— ✜ —————

Destiny of Man Without Divine Love Who Dies Only with Natural Love and Belief in the Creeds and Dogmas of the Churches – September 28, 1916 (I:86-90)

I Am Here. *Jesus.*

I come tonight to tell you that you are in a better condition to write than you have been for some time and I think it best that I deliver to you a message.

Well, I will write on the subject of the destiny of the man who has not the Divine Love in his soul, and dies with only the natural love and a belief in the creeds and dogmas of the churches. I know that many men believe that the creed of the churches is what is necessary for the salvation of mankind; I mean as to baptism and observance of the sacraments, and the belief that in my name men may be saved— are sufficient and all that are necessary to insure them an entrance into the Kingdom of Heaven; and in such belief rest, with the feeling of assurance that nothing else is required or in any way to be sought for and acquired.

The large majority of professing Christians are in this state of belief, and hence the greater number of mankind will not enter the Kingdom of Heaven, or become in their natures Divine. I have already told you what is the future of those who possess this Divine nature of the Father, and now I will confine my message to the future of this great majority.

As you may know, the river can never run higher than its source and neither can this majority attain to a perfection and happiness superior to that which was possessed by man before the time of the fall from the state of his perfect creation, and hence, no matter how great his progress may be in his natural love or in his moral or mental qualities, he can never excel the first created man as he was before the fall. And the only possible future for this vast majority is the condition and development that existed in the perfect man of God's first creation.

I know it is said that man has in him that which is a part of the Divinity of God, and that by his own efforts he may develop that Divine Substance until he becomes Divine himself, and of the nature of the Father. But this is not true, and it is not possible to develop the Divine Love or any essence of the Divine out of that which has not, in itself, there is nothing of the nature of the Divine. In the spirit world, and I mean the spiritual as well as Celestial, laws prevail, and are just as certain in their operations as are the laws of the material world and a fundamental law is, that only like produces like; although in the physical world it may appear that a derivative is not like that from which it is derived, but this is in appearance only, for in substance and essence the likeness exists and cannot be eradicated.

AND SO AS TO THE REAL CONDITION OF THE SOUL OF MAN, IF HE HAS ONLY THE NATURAL LOVE—THE CREATED LOVE—THE DEVELOPMENT OF THAT LOVE WILL RESULT IN THAT WHICH CANNOT POSSIBLY BE GREATER OR OTHER THAN THAT WHICH IN ITS CONSTITUENT PARTS IS ONLY THE NATURAL LOVE, AND NO MATTER WHAT THE PERFECTION MAY BECOME, THE DIVINE ELEMENT IS ABSENT, AND ALL THE LIMITATIONS THAT ARE INHERENT IN THE CREATED BEING STILL CONTINUE TO FORM A PART OF AND CONTROL THAT BEING.

There is a limit to the development of this natural love and to the state of happiness beyond which it is not possible for this being to go, and that limit is the qualities and excellence possessed by the first man before he became defiled and impregnated with sin. The mind of such being is also limited in the progress which it may make in obtaining knowledge, for that mind being a thing of creation is bound by the limitations that that creation imposed.

SO I SAY, SUCH A MAN CAN NEVER PROGRESS HIGHER THAN THOSE ATTRIBUTES OR QUALITIES WITH WHICH HE WAS ENDOWED WHEN HE WAS THE PERFECT MAN, EITHER SPIRITUALLY OR MENTALLY, UNLESS HE SEEKS FOR AND OBTAINS THE DIVINE LOVE. When spirits come and write that life in this spirit world is always progressive, these spirits who write have never attained to this limit of which I speak, and hence, to them, progression is endless; and this belief is very beneficial because it inspires them to make an effort to progress.

There are many spirits in this perfect state in the highest sphere of natural love or mentality, but they are spirits who have been in the spirit world for a vast number of years, and are what you might call ancient spirits. These spirits have realized this limitation of which I write, and while they can change the objects of their seeking and the sources of their happiness, yet their progress has its ending, and often there comes to them dissatisfaction and a realization that over and beyond their sphere, there must be something that may be obtained, that surpasses their perfect state and development. And as a result of this dissatisfaction, many of these spirits, in moments of their unrest, give heed to the suggestions of those spirits who have become possessed of the Divine Essence, and upon whom is no limitation of progress; for these latter spirits are at all times in the highest sphere of these spirits of perfected natural love [sixth sphere], trying to show them the way to the higher development and happiness of the Celestial Spheres.

It may seem surprising to you, but it is a fact, that these spirits of the natural love, during their periods of progression and especially as they make nearer approach to their perfection, in the satisfaction and happiness that they experience in that progression, will not listen to the spirits of the Divine Spheres, or believe that there can be any other methods of progress more desirable or excellent than the ones that they are pursuing, and only when they come to realize the dissatisfaction that I speak of, will awaken to the fact, or consent to be awakened to the fact, that there may be a way that leads to things beyond their limits of progress and the perfection that they may have acquired.

So, as I say, the higher the progress of these spirits and the farther away they advance from the earth plane, the greater the difficulty in persuading them that there is a state of perfection and happiness surpassing that which they are seeking for, and a way different from the way they are pursuing.

As these spirits progress in their natural love and in the development of their created minds, much happiness and satisfaction come to them, and in each stage of progress, so much greater do these experiences become, that they readily conceive that there can be no way superior to the one that they are travelling, and, hence, having such belief, the difficulty of convincing them to the contrary becomes almost insurmountable. As a consequence the spirits of the Celestial Spheres and those of the spirit spheres who are progressing in the Divine Love, give the great part of their time and efforts to convincing spirits of these higher truths while they are in the earth planes, before the happiness that I mention is experienced.

The life on earth and that in the earth planes of the spirit world are the states in which the souls of mortals and of spirits have the best opportunities for learning and believing these truths that show them the way to the progression that is without limitation or ending, and hence, the importance of men knowing these truths, and of spirits also, before they experience the satisfaction and pride, I may say, that the advancement in the development of their natural love and mental and moral qualities gives them.

UNTIL THE TIME COMES WHEN THE FATHER SHALL WITHDRAW FROM MAN AND SPIRIT THE PRIVILEGE OF OBTAINING THIS DIVINE LOVE AND ESSENCE, WHICH TIME WILL BRING THE SECOND DEATH, THESE SPIRITS AND ALL SPIRITS AND MORTALS WILL HAVE THE OPPORTUNITY OF SEEKING FOR AND FINDING THE WAY TO THE CELESTIAL SPHERES AND IMMORTALITY. BUT AFTER THAT TIME THIS PRIVILEGE WILL NO LONGER EXIST, AND THEN THOSE SPIRITS AND MORTALS WHO HAVE NOT FOUND AND FOLLOWED THE WAY OF THAT

PRIVILEGE, WILL BE AND BECOME ONLY THE PERFECT BEINGS, AS WERE THEIR FIRST PARENTS. THEY WILL HAVE NO ASSURANCE OF IMMORTALITY, OR EVEN CONTINUOUS LIFE, AND THAT DISSATISFACTION AND LONGING FOR SOMETHING UNKNOWN, WILL BE THEIRS.

They will remain only the created beings in spirit body, soul and mind, and as the first parents had all the qualities that these restored men will have, and fell, and why may it not be that they will fall? That there may come some change in the individualized spirit that will destroy that individuality and dissolve it into its elements of pre-creation? No spirit knows that such a change will take place, that the perfect spirit will not always retain the same individuality, or that the happiness of such spirit will not always exist. And neither does any spirit know that these things will continue to be.

THEN WHY SHOULD HE NOT CHOOSE THAT COURSE WHICH LEADS TO DIVINITY AND CERTAINTY OF IMMORTALITY AND PROGRESS, RATHER THAN THE ONE WHICH LEADS TO LIMITATION OF PROGRESS AND HAPPINESS, AND TO UNCERTAINTY OF IMMORTALITY?

I have written enough for tonight. I will come again soon. So remember that I love you and am with you trying to help you spiritually and that I pray to the Father to bless you. Goodnight. Your brother and friend,

Jesus.

Birth and Life of Jesus Up to His Public Ministry – June 7, 1915 (I:5-9)
I Am Here. *Jesus.*

I want to write to you tonight about my birth and life up to the time of my public ministry.

I was born in Bethlehem, as you know, in a manger, and when I was a few days old my parents took me to Egypt, in order to avoid the soldiers of Herod who were sent to destroy me, and who did kill a great number of male infants of less than two years of age. The Bible story of my birth and the flight of my parents and the murder of the innocents, is substantially correct; and I only wish to add to it, that when my parents arrived in Bethlehem they were not compelled to seek the manger of a stable in order that I might be born, on account of poverty, for they were supplied with funds and everything that was needed to make my birth comfortable for my mother; and as a matter of fact my father was not poor in the world's goods as poverty was considered in those days.

The Bible says the wise men came and brought offerings of gold and frankincense to my parents, or rather to me, but my parents have told me that it did not amount to so very much, so far as the money value of the same was concerned, and that their expenses of fleeing to Egypt was met by the funds that my father had prior to his reaching Bethlehem.

After they arrived in Egypt my father sought the home of a Jew, who was his relative, and lived there for a long time, doing the work that his trade fitted him to do; and by his work supported the family, and to an extent, educated myself and my brothers and sisters, for I had four brothers and three sisters, and were all, except myself, born in Egypt.

When I became of proper age, I attended the common school provided for small children, and was taught those things that had to do with the religion of the Jews, and some things that were not religious in their nature. I was never taught the philosophy of the Egyptians or of the other pagan philosophies; and when it is stated that I received my religious ideas or moral teachings from any of these philosophers, they are mistaken.

My education as to these matters of religion was derived from the teachings of the Old Testament, or rather from Jewish teachers whose text book was the Old Testament.

My development in the knowledge of the truths which I taught during my public ministry, was caused by my inner spiritual faculties, and my teacher was God, who, through His angels and through my soul perceptions, caused to come to me those truths or rather the knowledge of them, and in no other way did I obtain it.

I was not born with the knowledge that I was the son of God sent to earth to teach these great truths, or to announce to mankind the rebestowal of the great gift of immortality, and the means of acquiring it. But this knowledge of my mission came to me after I became a man and had the frequent communions with God by my spiritual senses.

I was never in the presence of the Jewish priests, expounding to them the law and asking questions when about twelve years of age, as stated in the Bible, and not before my first appearance, after I became a man, did I attempt to show priest or layman, that I was the messenger of the Father, and sent by Him to proclaim the glad tidings of immortality restored and of the great love of the Father which was necessary to make all men at one with Him, and to give them a home in His Kingdom.

I never was a sinful boy or man, and did not know what sin was in my heart; and strange as it may seem, I never sought to teach others these truths until after my mission was declared by John the Baptist.

In my boyhood days I was the same as other boys and engaged in the plays of childhood and had the feelings of a child, and never thought I was anything else than a child. In no wise was I different from other children, except in the particular that I have named, and any account of me to the contrary is untrue.

My teachings were those that the Father had committed to me from the beginning, but which I was only conscious of after I became a close communicant of the Father, and learned from Him my mission. So you must believe that I was a son of man as well as a son of God, and that in the literal sense. I would not have been true to my mission had I claimed that I was the only son of God, for it is not true—and men should not so teach it.

Yes, I know it was said that my mother was told of the object of my birth and what a blessed woman she was, but this is not true. My mother, as she has told me, had no reason to suppose that I was different from other children born of men. The story of the Angel of God coming to her and telling her that she must submit to the birth of a child who would be begotten by God or by His Holy Spirit, and that she, as a virgin, should bear and give birth to that child, is not true, for she never in all her life told me that she had any such visitor; and I know that she would be as much surprised, as are many men, that such a thing as the birth of a child by a virgin could take place. So you see the Bible account of my being begotten and all the attending circumstances are not true.

My father, Joseph, never supposed at any time that I was not his child, and the story of the angel coming to him and telling him that he must not put her away because of appearance is not true, because he never in all my conversations with him, intimated that I was other than his own child.

Between the time that I was twelve years of age and my public ministry, I lived at home with my parents, and assisted my father in his business of carpenter, and during all this time no hint ever fell from him that I was not his child, or that I was different from other children, except that I did not do sinful things.

When I commenced to get this divine love into my soul, I became very close to the Father, and this relationship resulted in my realizing that I was sent by God with a mission to perform and a great and important truth to declare; and, at last, the voice in my soul told me that I was my Father's true son and I believed it, and commenced to teach and preach the truths of His love bestowed and the salvation of men.

I knew John the Baptist when I was a child growing up. He was my cousin and we often played together, and afterwards discussed the truth of my mission and the way in which it should be made known to the world.

John was a great psychic and saw in his vision who I was and what my mission on earth was, and, hence, when the time came, he made the announcement of my coming. He realized the difference in our missions, and spoke of his not being worthy to unloosen my shoes. But, yet, he did not fully understand my mission and the great truth of the bestowal of immortality upon man by the Father.

I first became the Christ when I was anointed by my Father, and that occurred at the time of my baptism by John. I as Christ am different from myself as Jesus. Christ means that principle which the Father has conferred upon me, which made me at one with Him in the possession of this great love. Christ is that love itself made manifest in me as man. This Christ principle is universal and is everywhere, just as is the Holy Spirit, but I am limited in my place of occupancy just as you are.

I never as Jesus merely promised the great gift, mentioned in the Bible, such as, where two or three are gathered together there will I be also; for it would be impossible for me to be in all places at the same time. But Christ, being without form or limitation, is omnipresent and, consequently, may fulfill my promise in this regard. Christ is as much alive today as ever. He was never crucified and never died as did Jesus.

Well, I think you are too sleepy now to continue, well because you need sleep. I know of no special influence being exerted over you to produce sleep. I will continue in the near future. Your brother and friend,

Jesus.

————➤❉◄————

Authenticity of the Bible (I:150-154)
  I Am Here. *Luke. (St. Luke of the New Testament)*
  I desire tonight to write on the subject of "*What is the fact with reference to the authenticity of the Bible.*" I was with you at the lecture of the preacher on this subject, and was surprised that he could announce with such apparent confidence that the Bible is the authentic word of God, actually written by the men whose names appear therein as the writers of the same. The fact that he traced back the existence of certain manuscripts and versions to a hundred and fifty years subsequent to the time of the teachings of Jesus, did not establish the truth of his declaration that by such establishment the authenticity of the Bible, or the genuineness of the manuscripts as they now exist contain the real writings of the apostles, or of those persons who are supposed to be the writers of the same from the fact that their names are associated with these manuscripts.

  Neither is it true that John's life was prolonged to the end of the first century in order that he might write the true declarations of the eternal truths as described by Jesus, for John did not live until that time, and his writings were not preserved as he had formulated them, nor was the results of his declarations transmitted truthfully, as claimed by those who teach the inviolability of the scriptures.

  I was a writer upon these sacred subjects, and as I have before told you, I wrote a document which was called the "Acts of the Apostles", and left a number of copies of my writings when I died; but such compilation was merely a history of what I had heard from those who had lived with and heard the teachings of Jesus, and of their efforts to circulate and teach his doctrines after his death. I also had the benefit of some writings of the disciples about Jesus, but such writings were very few, for these disciples and followers of Jesus did not commence to place in the form of manuscript his teachings or the experience of his life until a long time after he had left the earth. They expected his speedy return when he would become their king and legislator, and hence, they saw no occasion or necessity for preserving in the form of writings the truths in which he had instructed them.

I know that after my own death the writings that I had left were not preserved intact, and that many things that I had incorporated therein, were in the numerous copying and recopyings of my manuscripts left out and ignored, and many things that I did not write and that were not in accord with the truth were inserted by these various successive copyists in their work of reproduction. And many of these omitted things and additions were of vital importance to the truth of things spiritual as they had been declared by the disciples as containing the truths that Jesus had taught.

And during the period—and the short period as the lecturer denominated it—between the earliest writings of the fathers of the church, and the times of the actual occurrences of the things to which these writings are supposed to relate and correctly describe, there were many changes made in the writings that I had left, as well as those left by the other original writers.

Even in epistles of Paul, which these theologians and Bible students claim have more authenticity and greater certainty than the gospels or other epistles of the Bible, many changes were made between the times of their writings and the times of the execution of the manuscripts or of the sermons of the fathers of the early church.

Within that one hundred and fifty years the truth of the spiritual teachings of the Master, had become, to a more or less extent, lost to the consciousness and knowledge of those who attempted to reproduce the original writings, because these men had become less spiritual, and their thoughts and efforts had become more centered in building up the church as a church than in attempting to develop and teach and preserve the great spiritual truths. The moral precepts became the dominating objects of their writings and teachings and were more easily comprehended by them than were precepts that taught the way to the development of their souls and to a knowledge of the will of the Father, and the mission of Jesus to mankind as a way-shower and savior of souls, rather than as a Messiah to establish his kingdom on earth.

No, I declare with authority the authenticity of the Bible cannot be established as the word of God, for in very many particulars it is not His word, but on the contrary, contains many assertions of truth that are not truths and diametrically opposed to His truths, and to Jesus's teachings of the truth.

The Bible has changed and perverted the whole plan of God for the salvation of man, and has substituted a plan that arose from the limited wisdom of those who attempted to convince mankind that they had a knowledge of God and of His designs as to the creation and destiny of man; and they were influenced very largely in this particular by their knowledge of the belief in the teachings of the Jewish church and the history of the Jewish race in its dealings with God, as they supposed, and in the teachings of the scribes and Pharisees. This fact was conspicuously shown by these writers attempting to substitute Jesus in their plan of salvation in the place of the animals in sacrifice in the Jewish plan of salvation. As the God of the Jews in order to be appeased and satisfactorily worshiped, demanded blood and more blood, so the God, that Jesus declared was the God of all the peoples of the earth, in order to be appeased and satisfactorily worshiped, demand blood and that the blood of His dearly beloved son.

Among these writings of the Bible there are many things declared to be truths, and embodied as the actual words of God, that are contradictory and unexplainable, and which, if they were the words of God, or even the teachings of Jesus, would contain no contradiction, or admit of any constructions that were not consistent one with the other.

As the additions and emasculations and interpretations were made in the original writings of those who declared the truths as they had heard them from the Master, the decreasing want of comprehension of spiritual things and the growing wisdom of their own finite intellects, caused them to conceive a plan on the part of God for man's salvation, and as the recopying continued the thoughts of those who copied, or who dictated the same, became more centered on this plan, and so these copies were gathered together and considered, and efforts to have some agreement in the declaration of this plan; and as the new copies were made they were constructed with the view of showing forth this agreement.

It must not be supposed that the copies from which the manuscripts that are the basis of the Bible were made were executed and preserved in a manner that caused them to be isolated one from the other, and that they were not all known to the persons who copied or caused the copying of the writings from which the manuscripts were made, for that would not be true. These, what may be called the basic copies, were in circulation at the time the Christian fathers wrote, and they had access to them, and quoted from them and helped to give them the interpretations that now prevail in the churches with the additional interpretations since those days.

Men know now that among these Christian fathers were bitter disputes as to what was a part of the word, and as to what should be accepted and what rejected among these writings antedating the manuscripts that form the basis of the Bible and that many manuscripts, purporting to be the word of God were rejected as such, and for the reason that they could not have been the records of God's word, because they did not agree with what the bishops of the church in their human knowledge and reason accepted as God's word should be. Even these bishops disagreed and differed, just as the human minds and reason disagree with one another.

Then I say the lecturer did not prove the authenticity of the Bible as being the word of God. He did not go down the stream of time as he called it, far enough to discover the existence of any authenticity, and that being so his argument of proof is just as weak as if he had started from the time of the printed Bibles, where their contents are substantially the same, but they not being the originals, the similarity proves nothing.

What I have said with reference to my own writings applies to the writings of all the others. The Bible does not contain their writings as they wrote and left them to humanity.

The Bible contains many truths, and enough to enable man to reach the Kingdom of Heaven provided they are correctly understood and applied, but there are so many things taught therein as truths, which are just the opposite of truth, that they make it difficult for men to discern and apply the truth, and comprehend the will of God with respect to men and the destinies that must be theirs according as they follow and obey that will or do not do so.

John has already written you on this subject with reference to his writings and so has Paul as to his, so that there is no necessity for me to deal with the errors and interpretations contained in their writings.

I will not write more now as you are tired, but will soon come and write a message on another subject that I have been desiring to write for some time. With my love and blessings, I am, Your brother in Christ,

Luke.

———⟫⟪———

Importance of the Jews Learning Jesus' Correct Teachings (I:260-262)
Moses, the Prophet of God of Ancient Days.

I have been with you on several occasions when some of the ancient spirits wrote you, and I was much interested. I am still the faithful servant of God, but in addition, a believer in Jesus, who is the greatest of all the sons of the Father, and the only one of all God's messengers who brought to light, life and immortality.

I could not have said this before his coming. I mean that I could not have said that other great reformers and teachers of the truths of God had not done this, because I did not know before the coming of Jesus what life and immortality meant—and no man or spirit before that time knew this great truth.

I am now in the Celestial Heavens with many of the old prophets and seers who have received this great gift of the Divine Love, and many who lived and died since Jesus' time are also Celestial spirits—partaking of immortality.

I now see that many of my teachings were not true—that love did not enter into them, but rather the spirit of retaliation which is absolutely no part of the truths of the Father. The Jews still look upon me as their great teacher and law-giver, and many of them observe literally my laws.

And I want to tell you this fact, because I believe that when you publish the messages of the Master, should you publish also what I may write, many Jews will believe me, and that I and many of those who taught my teachings, are now engaged in showing the spirits of Jews who come into the spirit world the truth as taught by the Master.

The Jewish nation is the most strict of all people in their beliefs in and observations of their religious doctrines as set forth in the Old Testament; and, hence, will be among the last of all men to accept the truths which I now understand and teach. But I hope that something which I may communicate to you will cause them to think and become believers and observers of this new revelation of the truth.

They have fought and suffered for their religion in all these centuries and are still doing so, and the one great thing that more than any other, has prevented them from accepting the teachings of Jesus and believing in his mission to mankind, is that his followers, or those who attempted to write his teachings, and those who interpreted the same, declare and maintain that Jesus is God—that the true God was three instead of one, as I in the Decalogue declared. This has been the great stumbling block to the Jews, and when they read, as they may, that Jesus himself declares and proclaims that he is not God but only his son, and that they are also his sons, they will look upon his teachings with more tolerance, and many of them will be inclined to accept his truths and the truths of the Father; and Judaism in its religious aspect will gradually disappear, and the Jews will become a part of the one great religious brotherhood of men, and as in our Celestial Heavens, there will be on earth no more Jew and no more Gentile, but all will become one in their belief in the Father and the mission of Jesus. He will be accepted as the Messiah not only of the Jew but of the whole world, and then God's chosen people will not be a very small minority of God's children, but the whole world will be his chosen people.

I am so interested in this phase of the great truths that shall be given to and accepted by men, because I was more than any other man responsible for the present beliefs of the Jews, which causes them to hold themselves separate and apart from all the rest of mankind as the chosen and specially selected of God's people.

I will not write more tonight, but I feel that I must ask you to permit me to write again, as I have a mission to perform on earth to undo a work which I so effectively performed when I was the leader of my people.

As Jesus is teaching and will teach all mankind the way to the Father and immortality, I must teach my people the way to get rid of these erroneous and false beliefs which are contained in the Old Testament. So, thanking you, I will say, goodnight.

Moses, the lawgiver of the Jews.

———— ❊ ————

Woman of Endor Was Not a Wicked Woman as Many Believe (I:287)
Saul of the Old Testament.

I am the same Saul that called up Samuel, or rather who caused the woman of Endor to do so.

I was a wicked man in those days, and knew not the love of God, and very little of my fellow mortals. I was a cruel man and a worker of iniquity, and violated God's laws in many ways.

As you have read, I came to the end of my resources and went to consult Samuel as the last resort. I did not know that God had abandoned me until Samuel had told me.

Yes, He did and was my protector as long as I obeyed Him and did what was right in His sight. I know that He did, because when I obeyed Him, I was successful and happy.

I only knew from what the prophets told me, and they claimed to have communications with God in some way. I believed this, and hence thought that God was protecting me.

I am a redeemed spirit now and am happy in the Love of the Father. I became a lover of the Father and an inhabitant of His Kingdom long after Jesus proclaimed the Great Truth of Divine Love restored. Before that I was a spirit who lived in the happiness which I experienced in developing my soul and becoming a good spirit, free from sin and error. But this happiness is not that which I now enjoy.

I want to confirm what Samuel said as to the woman of Endor. She was not a witch or evil woman, but was a medium and received communications from the higher spirits of the spirit world. She had been abused for centuries, and should not be further thought of as a wicked woman.

I will not write more tonight.

Well, do you suppose that we of the spirit world stand still in our mental advancement? I know all the important languages of the earth and can write them and understand them. Do not think that spirits do not learn here just as they learned as mortals. The only difference is that they can learn so much more rapidly and can retain their knowledge more easily than mortals can.

So I will say good night. Your brother in Christ,

Saul.

———※———

Genesis Copied from Ancient Writings on Creation and Fall of Man (I:284-6)

Leytergus. (Ancient Spirit)

I was a native of Arabia and lived before the time of Abraham, the Jewish patriarch.

I come to you tonight to tell you that before the Jewish Testament was written, I had written a book containing a description of creation and of the fall of man, and that the book of Genesis was copied after my writings, which were founded on traditions older than were the description of Genesis.

These descriptions of the creation of the world were not the works of men inspired by the angels or by any other instrumentalities of God, but were the results of the imaginations of the minds of men who lived long before I lived, and who left only tradition of their writings or teachings. I say all this to show you that the world has existed for many thousands of years longer than the account of its creation in the Jewish Scriptures would lead you to think.

I don't know when it was created and I have not found any spirit in the spiritual world who does know. Of course no spirit would know of his own knowledge because in the natural order of things, man must have been created subsequent to the creation of those things which were necessary for his sustenance and comfort. I have never seen any angels who were not at one time mortals, and hence I could not learn from them when the world was created and I have never seen any angels or spirits to whom God has made this revelation. So I say the creation of the world or rather any account of it is all a matter of speculation and tradition.

Yes, I have been informed as to the fall of man. My information is as follows:—

When man was created he was made two-fold—that is, there were male and female beings—which was intended to make a perfect one without losing any individuality on the part of either. Their names were not Adam and Eve, but Aman and Amon, which meant the male Am and the female Am. Am meaning the exalted creation of God.

These beings were made perfect physically and spiritually. But these souls were not possessed of all the qualities of the Great Creator Soul, and in that particular were inferior to the Great Creator. But as regards this soul part of their creation, they were made in the image of their Creator. The physical or spiritual part of their creation was not in the image of their Creator, for He had no physical or spiritual body. But their soul part was only made in the image of their Creator— and not of the Substance—but this image was given a potentiality of obtaining or receiving the Substance of the soul qualities of their Creator and provided, if they pursued that course in their existence or living which would cause their souls to receive, in accordance with certain operations of the laws which their Creator had prescribed, this soul Substance. And only in obedience to these laws or their operations could this Substance of the Creator Soul, be obtained.

Well, these creatures were not equal to the test, or rather requirements, and after living awhile they became possessed of the idea that they needed not to comply with these prescribed laws, but could of their own will and power obtain this Substance by doing that which they had been forbidden by these laws to do, and so in their efforts to obtain this Substance or Divine Love they disobeyed these laws, and, as a consequence, these potentialities of obtaining the Substance of the Creator Soul were taken from them, and then they became beings still possessed of the spiritual and physical forms and continued souls, but not of these great potentialities—and this was the fall of man.

The story of the apple is a myth. No apple or anything else that was intended to be eaten, formed any part of the fall. It was wholly the fall of the soul's potentialities.

THE DISOBEDIENCE WAS THE GREAT UNLAWFUL DESIRE ON THE PART OF THESE TWO, TO OBTAIN THIS SOUL SUBSTANCE BEFORE, IN ACCORDANCE WITH THE OPERATIONS OF THE LAWS PRESCRIBED, THEY WERE FITTED OR IN CONDITION TO RECEIVE IT; AND AS A CONSEQUENCE, THEY BECAME DISOBEDIENT, AND BEING POSSESSED OF WILLS WHICH WERE NOT IN ANY WAY BOUND OR LIMITED BY THEIR CREATOR, THEY EXERCISED THESE WILLS IN ACCORDANCE WITH THEIR DESIRES, AND FROM THIS DISOBEDIENCE THE WILLS OF MEN AND WOMEN HAVE CONTINUED TO ACT IN ACORDANCE WITH THEIR DESIRES AND IN VIOLATION OF THE GREAT LAWS OF TRUTH, WHICH WERE MADE FOR THE TWO CREATURES AT THE TIME OF THEIR

CREATION AND ARE THE SAME UNCHANGEABLE LAWS OF THIS TIME.

THE SOUL SUBSTANCE THAT THESE TWO FORFEITED WAS THE DIVINE LOVE OF THEIR CREATOR, WHICH, HAD THEY BY THEIR OBEDIENCE BECAME POSSESSED OF, WOULD HAVE MADE THEM A PART OF HIS DIVINITY, AND THENCE LIKE HIM NOT ONLY IN IMAGE BUT IN SUBSTANCE AND REALITY.

THE POTENTIALITY THAT WAS TAKEN FROM THEM WAS THE PRIVILEGE WHICH THEY HAD TO OBTAIN THIS SOUL SUBSTANCE OR DIVINE LOVE BY COMPLYING WITH OEDIENCE WHICH THESE LAWS PRESCRIBED. SO YOU SEE THE STORY OF GENESIS IS MERELY SYMBOLICAL.

I have nothing further to say tonight.

I love in a sphere which is part of the Celestial Heavens. I have, through the mercy of God and His gift, declared by Jesus, received this potentiality and through it the Soul Substance which our first parents forfeited.

The name which I have given you was mine when on earth. It is Arabic and nothing else. You must know, that many of the names of my time, were in after centuries incorporated in the nomenclature of other nations and races.

So I will say good night. Your brother in Christ,

Leytergus.

The Only Prayer Needed – December 2, 1916 (I:40-2)

I Am Here. *Jesus.*

I merely want to say a word for the benefit of you and your friend [Leslie R. Stone], and that is, that I have listened to your conversation tonight, and find that it is in accord with the truth; and the influence of the Spirit is with you both. Continue in your line of thought and in prayer to the Father, and, also, in your making known to others, whenever the opportunity arises, the importance of seeking for and getting the Divine Love.

As your friend [Celestial spirit] said, the only prayer that is necessary is the prayer for the inflowing of this Love; all other forms, or real aspirations, of prayer are secondary, and of themselves, will not tend to produce this Love in the souls of men.

Let your prayer be as follows:—

[THE PRAYER PERFECT]

Our Father, in the Celestial Heaven, we recognize You as all Holy, loving and merciful, and we, as Your children, are not the subservient or depraved creatures false teachers would have us believe. We are the greatest and most wonderful of all Your creations, and the objects of Your great soul's love and tenderest care.

Your will is that we become at-one with You, and partake of the great love bestowed upon us through Your mercy and desire that we become, in truth, Your children through love, not through the sacrifice and death of any of Your creatures.

We pray that You will open up our souls to the inflowing of Your love, and then will come the Holy Spirit to bring into our souls Your Divine Love in great abundance, until we are transformed into the very essence of Yourself. Then will come to us such faith as will cause us to realize that we are truly Your children, and one with You in very substance, and not in image only. Give us such faith as will cause us to know that You are our Father, the bestower of every good and perfect gift, and that only we, ourselves, can prevent Your love changing us from a mortal into an immortal.

Let us never cease to realize that Your love is waiting for each and all of us, and that when we come to You in faith and earnest aspiration, Your love will never be withheld from us.

Keep us in the shadow of Your love every hour and moment of our lives and help us to overcome all the temptations of the flesh, and the influence of the powers of the lower ones, which so constantly surround us and endeavor to turn our thoughts away from You to the pleasures and allurements of this world.

We thank You for Your love and the privilege of receiving it. We know You are the loving FATHER who smiles upon us in our weakness, and is always ready to help us, and take us to Your arms of love.

We pray this with all the earnestness and sincere longings of our souls, and trusting in Your love, give You all the glory, honor and love that our finite souls can give. Amen

This is the only prayer that men need offer to the Father. It is the only one that appeals to the love of the Father, and with the answer, which will surely come, will come all the blessings that men may need, and which the Father sees are for the good of His creatures.

I am in very great rapport with you tonight, and see that the Father's love is with you, and that your souls are hungry for more. So, my brothers, continue to pray and have faith, and in the end will come a bestowal of the love like unto that which came to the apostles at Pentecost.

I will not write more now. In leaving you, I will leave my love and blessings and the assurance that I pray to the Father for your happiness and love. Good night. Your brother and friend,

Jesus.

ABOUT THE AUTHOR

PATRICIA DOYLE HAS been studying consciousness and the afterlife since the early 1960's after a manifestation at a *séance* led her to pursue spiritual truth with cautious enthusiasm. She was agnostic in 1974 when she had an NDE and was enveloped in God's Love and Presence. In 1976, she had a transformative experience with Jesus, and was astonished when invited to participate in the revealing of his second coming. Six years later, when introduced to the messages through Padgett, Jesus visited her again to verify them. Two years later, she was appointed president of the Foundation dedicated to these profound messages.

Patricia's NDE was published in *Searchlight* in 2012 by the Academy for Spiritual and Consciousness Studies. In 2013, her essay, "Encounter with God: Prophecy, Spiritualism and the Old Testament," appeared in the *Journal for Spiritual and Consciousness Studies*. She retired from the University of Puget Sound as Coordinator of the Physics Department and Dual-Degree Engineering Program. You can reach her at secondnewtestament@gmail.com.

INVITATION TO PARTICIPATE

THANK YOU IMMENSELY for taking the time to read this book. If you feel moved to help get the word out, the best way would be by leaving a review on Amazon. Every review is important. It's the number one thing that helps people decide whether to get a book. Please take a few minutes now to leave an honest review at amazon.

The more people who know about these simple, yet effective teachings of Jesus, the faster we can transform the fear-based world around us into a Love-based world. You will find several websites devoted to the Padgett messages by doing a simple Google search. You can also go the Foundation's website at http://secondnewtestament.org.

Dozens of my friends and colleagues from the Divine Love community are committed to bringing awareness of these teachings to the world. We represent a wide variety of Divine Love ministries, all working for the same goal of enlightening humanity to conscious possession of God's Love. Eva Peck, author and friend, compiled an extensive resource of individuals and organizations connected with the Padgett messages. It can be accessed at http://universal-spirituality.net/wp-content/uploads/2019/12/Divine-Love-Resource-Guide-1-2020.pdf.

We often have retreats filled with Divine Love prayer circles, presentations about the teachings, fun outings, and feasts of food and friendship. Many ideas and projects are shared to support one another in our spiritual growth and the furtherance of our common mission. Friends come from several international locales to take part in these empowering, Love-filled gatherings. We come together because Divine Love changed us and our individual searches for truth led us to these messages.

A passion project of mine is the creation of a Lighthouse Chapel with dichroic pigmented glass. A Foundation museum will be incorporated within the chapel as a public education venue. The chapel will host events like weddings, memorial services, and retreats. My goal is to manifest the Lighthouse Chapel within the next five years and to host a public Divine Love Uprising as an opening celebration. If you want to donate to the project, you can do so at http://secondnewtestament.org/store.html. Fifty percent of the profits from this book will go toward the Lighthouse Chapel.

If you would like to learn more about our activities or future books, drop me a line and provide your contact information at secondnewtestament@gmail.com.

Thank you!

Made in the USA
Columbia, SC
01 January 2025

50953754R00126